Chu Jeng

Books by Kevin B. Shearer

Chu Jeng
Book One of The Dragons of Wulin

Tenju Gen
Book Two of The Dragons of Wulin

Rume Lak
Book Three of The Dragons of Wulin

Han Erh
Book Four of The Dragons of Wulin

Torin Feng
Book Five of The Dragons of Wulin

Senya Dain
Book Six of The Dragons of Wulin

Gis Erh
Book Seven of The Dragons of Wulin

Return of The Wizard

Voyage of the Bád Dragain

Avalon

Excalibur

Camelot Armageddon

The Perfect Shadow

Chu Jeng
The Iron Fist

Book One of The Dragons of Wulin

To my wife, children, students and many teachers.
Without your inspiration the miracles would have never happened.

Forward:

Please keep in mind that these stories of the Seventeen Dragons of Wulin are not true stories. Furthermore, many of the elements in the stories are fanciful, exaggerated and/or impossible, which should make the metaphorical nature of these teaching stories obvious. Likewise; all characters, names and situations appearing in this work are fictitious. Any resemblance to real persons, living or dead, is purely coincidental. These stories are not intended as teaching manuals and you should not try to imitate anything you read here. Nor do they take place in China or Japan or any other place you could find on a map. These stories are told in an ancient tradition of removing as many cultural markers as possible so that every reader might see them as his or her own, though they do keep to a general oriental feel.

Many of the things believed by the characters in the stories are of a mystical or magical nature and do not reflect the beliefs of the author or those who teach and study Wind Fist Kung Fu. These tales are simply inspirational stories, which are designed to entertain readers and to illustrate some of the philosophies, practices and moral teachings of our unique and powerful fighting system and Tong Brotherhood.

So, we hope you simply enjoy the stories for what they are, and find your life richer for having read them.

CHU JENG

1 – INCEPTION

I was not always a Dragon.

In the fertile province of Gurin near the region of the five lakes there stood a prosperous village. I was born on a farm near that village into the family of Chu. My father gave me the name, Jeng. The village is gone now; burned by the Emperor's troops and the people slaughtered. Folk of the region are forbidden by law to speak the name of my family's village. I speak it now; Sanjurra.

The Dragon's Path called me away from that village just before the autumn harvest of my thirteenth year, though I could not have understood it then. It beckoned most cruelly with the murder of my beloved Uncle Senji, and that is how the whole thing started.

The air was cool with the morning mist not yet burned away by the sun as I walked toward the village with two buckets of yams to trade for wheat flour. I smiled at a memory of wrestling with Uncle Senji as I walked past his old farm on my way to the village. My father had many brothers and sisters, most of whom lived in or near the village, but I was an only child.

I had hoped to see my favorite uncle in town when I got to the market. He always made it to market before most of the other villagers, setting up the general area for them. The night before, he had promised me a small share in his profits if I stayed to help him for a few hours. It seemed a day like any other sweet autumn day until I neared the town circle where the sellers gathered.

Even before I entered the market circle, I knew by the noise of the crowd that there had been trouble. One of the village Elders shouted above the crowd. It sounded like the old widower and chief of the Elders, Korenda. His deep voice carried a plea across the angry mob. "No! We must call for a provincial investigator to prosecute this murder, and not let anger rule our decisions."

I was instantly saddened and yet curious, in the way that children so often are, to hear that another murder had occurred. I pressed closer to hear the details, and perhaps, get a glimpse. I had never seen a dead man.

Another Elder shouted, "No! An investigator will just haul away more of our youth for provincial or imperial service."

"Or slavery!" a woman warned, failing to choke back her frustrated sobs.

A more youthful voice made its way to the top of the din with, "The foreign Emperor and his puppet regional governors are vampires! We don't want their unholy help! They brought the bandits and warlords with them!"

"Down with the Tardor Emperor and up with the old dynasty of the Hahn people!" a teenage voice shouted. His treasonous patriotism frightened most of the crowd into an abrupt hush.

Taking advantage of the sudden quiet, Elder Korenda said, "We are all wounded by the untimely death of one of our most honored villagers. Let us not add more innocent blood to that of our friend Senji by throwing stones at the imperial hornet's nest. Bandits and highway thugs are the enemy. It is foolish to word-stab at the warlords, governors and Emperor."

My vision went gray and my head began to swim in a fog of grief. I did not want to believe what I had just heard, and my small stature prevented me from seeing for myself. Arguments continued as I dropped my yams and blindly pushed my way through the bigger people who were soon to decide the fate of my village and my life. At length, I stood looking at the slashed and motionless body of my father's brother. Uncle Senji had taught me to read and write. He had taught me to look for the deeper meaning in every word and even to marvel in the intricacies of a

2

simple leaf. He had been the big brother I never had and a wise and gentle friend whenever I needed him. He was gone forever. Leaving my load of yams behind, I ran all the way home and skirted Uncle's farm by cutting through the woods. The wailing of my uncle's widow and daughters reached out to me even through the trees, and cut right through my hands as I pressed my palms against my ears. Their cries struck me and killed a part of my childhood. Suddenly I took to my heart the worried and regret-filled words the grown people had been speaking above my head for years. So often, they had talked of happier times of health and prosperity for my village and the surrounding farms. They whispered nervous curses at the coming of the Tardor conquerors and their greedy Emperor from the north. They said the swarms of bandits, thieves and highway thugs were once rare in our region. Then the criminals prospered and the people suffered under the heels of the Tardor.

I ran on through the woods, crying and cursing myself for being an ignorant child and not listening to my elders. Before my father was born, his father had predicted that the outlaw gangs would someday form into armies of extortion, slavery and death. He was true in his thinking; for the most powerful gang bosses became warlords. We, the little people, were trapped beneath that triad of oppression. I wondered how I could have ignored the pain of my people. I cursed myself for being such a stupid child. And so, the murder of my Uncle Senji happened at the end of my thirteenth year and brought with it the death of my childhood.

By the time I reached my home, I had wiped the tears from my face and prepared myself to stand strong for my parents. The terrible news, however had already reached my father. His restrained grief was too much for me to bear and I hid myself outside near the wood pile. Later that night, some of the village Elders came to speak with my father.

Mother offered the men tea, but they politely refused, Elder Gazen saying, "We can't stay for long, Mrs. Chu. We're here to summon your husband to a village council to discuss the problem of regional banditry."

"I'm not an Elder," Father said.

Elder Kwan told him, "You're summoned because you've lost your brother to robbers." He shook his head slowly and added, "I'm terribly sorry about his death, my friend, and we offer our sincerest condolences to you and your family. All families who have lost loved ones to thugs in recent years will be represented at the council."

Elder Gazen said, "Our village has come to a sorry state since the better time of our grandfathers."

"What do you feel we can do about it?" Father asked.

3

Elder Kwan said, "I'm not sure. It's not only an evil situation, but an unnatural one we suffer. I have heard of distant kingdoms where the governing powers press very hard upon the people and also suppress thuggery. I have heard also of kingdoms rampant with banditry because the governing powers are weak and timid. Never in any tale have I heard of a land like ours, where the people suffer both stifling, intrusive tyranny *and* rampant crime."

Elder Gazen added, "The Emperor only punishes those criminals who cut in on his take of peasant blood. It is the same for the regional warlords."

Father said, "Perhaps it is time to carry death and destruction to the bringers of death and destruction. The powers of Heaven must be waiting for us to act on behalf of our own selves to throw off the burden of this unnatural situation." He hugged my mother and left with the Elders.

I had never heard my father talk like that before. He had always been a quiet and reserved man. Always so thoughtful and gentle with my mother and me, while kind and hospitable to all others.

I slept at my mother's side that night. I say I slept, but I did more worrying and thinking than sleeping. I was afraid with just the two of us there–afraid in my own family home for the first time in my life. It seemed suddenly that our house was made of the lightest paper and that thugs would burst in upon us at any moment. I wondered what I would do if bad men did come for us in the night—men with weapons and knowledge of warfare! We were simple farmers. I knew nothing of the war arts, though I had heard a few odd tales of war art masters. The things I had heard loomed in my mind and exaggerated my fears of the thugs I imagined circling the house of my father's fathers. I felt sick and knew I was nobody who could defend my mother or myself.

My father did not return home until late the next afternoon. His face was drawn and weariness had stooped his shoulders. My mother had a pot of rice and smoked fish waiting for him. She served him and questioned him while he ate.

"The end of our misery may be in sight," he told her.

"Those are words of hope, my dear, but I see no hope in your eyes."

"That's because danger weakens my hope. Come here and sit beside me, Jeng. The elders' plan involves you. You must hear what I have to say now."

It was the first time my father had called me to table with him still eating. I had not expected such a sign of manhood so long before I reached my sixteenth birthday. I sat down obediently and said nothing. My father

4

looked into my eyes with what seemed to be a mixture of pride, fear and grief. Mother beamed with a pride that almost hid her nervousness.

"We may have to send you out into the world, my son. It will be hard for you, because you will be alone in the world to represent our family name and our village." He ignored Mother's near swoon and continued, "Would you be frightened if we asked you to travel that way for us?"

"No!" my mother said. For a moment I thought she was answering for me.

"No," I blurted out, parroting her without thinking.

Then my father put his great calloused hand on my shoulder and said, "I am proud of you, son. I feared for you and thought you too much a child for the coming trial. But here you are just three years before your passage and showing the heart of a man. Even your eyes show some fire of manhood. Yes, son. Either today you have come to strength or I have never looked before."

"No," my mother said again. "He's only a boy. What are the Elders planning for my Jeng?"

Father rubbed his face with both hands and sighed. Then he looked at my mother and said, "All the youth of our village and farms are to be tested. The strongest twenty of our youth will be sent out into the world to learn a war art and bring it back to us one year later. Then a second testing will determine who has the best art. He with the best war art will teach the others. They will then teach all our youth to protect our people from bandits."

"Jeng is only a boy!" My mother began to cry openly.

Thinking back to those times, I feel that she overprotected me because I was her only child. She had conceived other children after me, but they all died at birth. I think Father felt the same about his tenuous family line, but he wanted me to grow up strong rather than protected into frailty.

Then Father said something to comfort my mother, and his words hurt my pride. "All the youth of our people will be tested. Jeng is to be included because his favorite uncle was murdered. No one expects him to be sent along with the twenty." His words filled me with bitterness and resolve. Turning to me, he squeezed my shoulder and said, "Chu Jeng, this is your chance to show the village the kind of family you come from. Though you are too young to have much of a chance of earning the commission of the village Elders, you can prove yourself to all." I nodded my agreement in silence and wanted to shout that I could do as well as anyone in the village or surrounding farms.

"Will the testing be dangerous?" my mother asked, calmer now. She was hoping for my failure! I could see it in her eyes along with relief. Relief! In her eyes I had already placed last in the test. I would be her shamed little porcelain doll, safe at home while other, better young men, carried the burdens of my people. They who could not possibly know the pain I felt on the day of my uncle's murder would carry my burden for me. I felt as if I were going to burst.

Father said, "The tests will be constructed over the next few days by the Elders. Then the young men of our area will be tested for their strength, perseverance, devotion to our people, intelligence, literary skills and endurance. The best will leave individually on the first day of spring. Those with many strong sons will assist the families who have given up their own sons for the quest. It is a desperate measure for our village to take, but there's nothing else we can do. I was surprised the Elders consented to it, but many angry voices were calling for even tougher action."

They sent me to bed that night without ever asking me how I felt about the whole matter. I did not think too harshly about them, though. I knew adults had their own ways of thinking and I had mine. I determined that I would qualify for the quest. I had never before felt so resolved in spirit as I did that night. I was unable to sleep at all, but lay in bed trying to think of ways to overcome the limitations of my small size and inexperience. I thought about some of the young men and boys of Sanjurra. Then I thought of Han Erh, the strong handsome farmer's son. He was labeled as prime choice of every eligible girl in the village. Han Erh was the sort of man who naturally and easily did everything better than everyone else. He did not even have the flaw of pride. I had always admired him, but that night I thought of him as my competition. Every time I imagined myself doing well in some test, Han Erh appeared in my visions and kindly showed me to be a childish oaf. My only hope was that there were twenty to be sent out next spring. My fear was that Han Erh was not the only villager in the contest who was much stronger, faster and smarter than I.

2 - QUEST

Three days later, my tension increased almost enough to throw me into despair. The people were gathered in the village circle to hear what the tests would be. I was stunned at the descriptions. Then I noticed the look on Han Erh's face off to my right. Though steadfastly impassive as ever, a glint of apprehension showed clear in his eyes. He noticed my stare and turned slightly toward me. I guess he read the horrified look on my face and smiled down at me as would a big brother; enough like Uncle Senji might have that it startled me.

"You don't have to pass every test," he whispered to me. "Just place in the top twenty. Do your best for your uncle Senji. Win or lose, you must honor him by doing a good job." After staring at my face, he added with a nod, "You will honor him."

After thinking about what he had said I was somehow released from the bulk of my fears. I nodded and smiled the most adult smile I could muster. He raised an eyebrow and turned back toward the Elders. From that point on, I no longer looked at him as an adversary. I decided to watch him and do whatever he did. I would even try to talk to him as much as possible and maybe think like he did, if I could. The few words he had spoken to me had already helped me to believe I could be more than an amusing child in the eyes of my people.

The time of testing turned out to be the hardest winter of my life. I ran, lifted heavy things, jumped, balanced, climbed, pushed, pulled and struggled against my fellow competitors until I thought my muscles would bleed right through my skin. The competitors also had to solve mental puzzles and were questioned about what we would do in certain difficult situations. We listened to long rambling lectures from the Elders and a few local philosophers they had brought to our village. It was often difficult to stay awake. Afterward we had to answer questions or even write essays about what they had said. Early on, several good boys complained about some of the tests. The Elders immediately threw the complainers out of the competition, much to their shame. I always watched my competitors closely whenever I could and learned from their mistakes, often just in time to avoid my own disasters. I was given no special consideration for being young and small, either by the Elders or my competitors. Perhaps it was the other boys who first thought I might have a chance of placing among the twenty. The Elders did not pay much attention to me other than to occasionally tell me how well I was honoring my uncle Senji. Only toward the end did they come to realize I might make it. I pushed myself beyond any limits I had previously known and my running speed, agility and endurance made up for my lack of strength. My determination and devotion countered my lack of knowledge and fledgling literary skills. Oh, how often I silently thanked my dear uncle for having taught me to read and having taught me so many other things that proved useful in the competitions.

When it was all over, Han Erh placed first among the competitors, much to everyone's expectations. Though last among us, I placed among those who were to be sent, much to everyone's surprise and certainly to my mother's horror.

"We can't let him go out there with the others," she said to my father. "He's just a boy." Again she used that word that I had come to hate when applied to me. I wondered why she had not seen the changes in me over the long hard winter.

My father truly did not want to send me off either, but his pride in my placing among the chosen was obvious. Even my mother saw it, though he tried to hide it from her. "We cannot act against the decision of the Council," he said. "They didn't want to send him either. Nobody expected him to do so well, but he did. Now we are held bound to the decision our Elders have taken. No family wants to give up their son, especially when planting is about to start. If we were to insist that Jeng stay home, all the other families will raise their own objections, and the whole plan will be ruined. There is nothing we can do, now, my dear woman. Jeng must leave with the others after the spring festival."

My mother raised a long string of objections and my father logically thwarted each objection. In the end she just wept and refused to talk to him. I was filled with both fear and excitement about the quest. During the winter of testing, I had grown in confidence and strength. I felt like there was nothing I could not do. I crept out of my house that night and walked toward Han Erh's house while my parents slept. Han Erh was standing near the crossroads by the old mill. He stood looking up at the moon.

"Hello, Jeng," he said in his usual friendly manner.

"Hello Erh," I said. "You can't sleep either?"

"I could if I wanted to. I just want to look around here without a lot of people talking and giving me unwanted advice. The teachers and testers have given me more than I can hold already."

He looked like a perfect statue of manliness in the moonlight. I almost ached inside with the desire that I could be a man like him when I grew up. "I know what you mean," I said. "Sometimes I stay awake at night, not to study, but to get some peace. Despite all that, I am going to miss this place. Heck, I'm going to miss all the places around here. It seems like you're feeling the same way, Erh."

He lowered his gaze and asked, "Will you promise to keep a secret, Jeng?"

"Absolutely, Erh."

"All right. I know you're young, but… well, have you ever been in love?"

"Yes. I was a couple of times," I answered quietly after a pause. "But I never told anyone and now you have to keep my secret."

Han Erh gave me a strange look and said, "My first cousin, Han Rinya, and I…" He struggled for words. "We can't ever marry, of course, but for three years…" Again he paused. "Well, we have exchanged vows of love, Jeng. She is so easy to be with and to tell how I feel about things. She feels the same about me." Erh grew quiet for a while and seemed to struggle with some inner thought, then said, "Her father wants her to marry Gener Chig. Gener Chig, of all people!"

"How terrible!" I blurted. "Of all the people!"

Erh nodded and continued. "I have helped her to avoid the arrangement thus far, but when I'm gone; what then? My parents have been wanting me to marry for a long time, but it's easier for a man to refuse. What's going to happen to her? I feel like I'm abandoning t5he sweetest person I've ever known."

"I'm very sorry about that Erh,"

I had never heard Han Erh speak so many words at one time. I could understand his feelings. Gener Chig, the merchant's son and only child, was as rich in material wealth as he was poor in compassion or of any really human feelings. He was probably the richest young man in the immediate region, and the poorest in true friends. He had plenty of toadies waiting for scraps from his golden table, but even they hated his haughty, overbearing attitude. I felt for Erh's predicament. Han Erh did not know, but it was one of his little sisters I had a desperate longing for, even then. Han Erh was also fairly rich by my family's standards. His family farm was a bit larger than most and his father even owned three splendid horses. But Erh never acted like more than a good, honest, hardworking farmer. Neither did his father or his brothers. Leaving home was bad enough without my friend Han Erh having to suffer his particular plight. I tried to change the subject.

"Erh, have you ever traveled far away?"

"No. Of course not."

"Are you afraid of the outside world?"

"No, Jeng. I'm not afraid. I just don't know exactly how I am going to complete the quest."

"The Elders told us all about how to travel safely and find a good master," I reassured him.

Han Erh turned to me and laughed softly. "Which of the Elders has traveled more than thirty miles from this village? Eh? None of them. They mean well, but they know little more than we do about the outside world."

"What should we do then?" I asked. I had come to know Han Erh's advice to be infallible during the months of hard testing and training. If anyone could know what to do it would be him.

He thought for a few minutes and said, "I'm not sure. I think I'll follow your plan. During the testing, you watched others and learned from them, often without asking a single question. I only know how to live well in our village. I think I'll watch outsiders and see how they live in the outside world."

I was honored that he might consider following my example in anything. "That's what I was planning to do," I replied. It was my plan, in an instinctive way I supposed. At least I had no better plan.

He smiled a knowing smile at me and tousled my hair. "Go home and get some sleep," he said. "The festival is tomorrow and then we leave."

I walked a few paces away and turned to face him again. "Han Erh. Will you win the fighting contest when we return?"

"I don't know," he said. "I only want to do my best and honor my family."

As I walked home, I knew that I was very different from Han Erh. He always excelled with ease and was lavished with honor. I had always struggled with every fiber of my being for any excellence I could achieve, and I was usually bested by bigger, stronger boys. He wanted only to do his best. I wanted desperately to win for once in my life; to win it all and conquer.

My mother had to call me three times before I awoke the next day. I should have started my day early and been filled with excitement. Instead, I was calmer than I could ever remember feeling. The cold, factual, steadiness of my own resolve was something entirely new to me, but I liked it instantly. I liked it very much. Perhaps I had used up all my excitement in the previous three days. Or perhaps Han Erh's words had changed me again. My mother stared oddly at me when I came to breakfast. I did not know if it was my quiet demeanor or if she stared because she thought she was losing me. I think I felt that too. My whole

10

world was slipping through my fingers, and I let it go so calml ̇ ̆ though I had no idea what strange new world might replace it. F it seemed that I could no longer see myself in that childish way ᴏ supposing I was the center of the world. I thought I stood at the edge of something great, not knowing if I could fit in or even ever come to understand it. If I could survive to bring no shame or grief upon my family, perhaps then, that would be enough, but I wanted so much more than that.

Even at the spring festival, where my fellows of the quest and I were the focus of honor, I mostly stayed in the background. My father, mother and cousins tried to bring me into the crowds and into the traditional contests. But I had withstood enough of contests and mass attention over the winter. I noticed Han Erh trying to avoid the praise and celebration being heaped upon him. I had a better chance of disappearing into the background though. Erh was always a sort of celebrity, despite his efforts not to be. Others of our number were quiet while some, like the potter's son, Denju Rehn, blossomed in the light of their newly acquired popularity. Denju was the only young villager we commonly referred to by his surname. His given name, Rehn, did not fit him as well as his family name, which means rock. He had only one sister and no brothers or cousins, so we could use his surname without risk of confusion. Denju was demonstrating how he came to place first in the rock lifting contest. It was one of the very few contests where Han Erh had not bettered everyone else. Denju lifted a pony on his back and walked around the town circle with shiny muscles bulging for all at the festival to see. Most of the villagers bet that he could not do it. They lost.

Bets were laid on the whole group of us chosen for the quest. Who would come home first? Who would be the best? Who would not return home? I wanted no part of it. I did not even want to hear it. It was a frenzy of gambling greater than any ever seen in the village before. Young men's names were called out and purses jingled in wild fervor and pride. My father loudly placed a large bet that I would come and be the victor in the fighting contest of the next spring festival. He smiled and nodded at me, but I could see that it was only money thrown away for my encouragement. I smiled back and turned to walk away from the frenzied gambling. Then it came to my mind that my father was the only person I had heard lay a bet on my success. He was a poor man who worked very hard for his money. As I walked, I remembered how generous he had always been with my mother and me. But I had never seen him waste even a half copper on gambling or even on himself. I turned to see him still

11

..aring after me. I had always loved my father, but in that moment I came to respect him and even revere him for the good man he was.

The next morning, we men of the quest said farewell to our families. Though I was a little afraid to leave and knew I would miss my parents, I made the parting short. I knew I would not be able to see my mother's tears for long and not shed my own. And it would not be right if I did cry. I was, for the first time in my life, counted among men to walk a man's road. It was enough that I was the smallest and youngest. Tears were absolutely out of the question. I walked toward the town circle with my left hand on the money belt my mother had sewn for me and hidden beneath my tunic. It was reassuringly heavy. I felt like the richest young man in the whole region.

When I reached the circle, most of my fellows were already there. The Elders had prepared a traveling bundle for each of us. When the last of us arrived, each of the Elders took a turn giving us advice and instructions. Our bundles contained food, clothes, money, bedding, letters of introduction and a small fighting knife. The village blacksmith had stamped his sign on the ends of the knife hilts along with some of the ancient symbols for good luck. Everything was in place and the coming of Sanjurra's destiny was all up to us. The Elders dismissed the gathering with wishes for good luck and a prayer for our safety. For a moment we all just stood there with the bundles hanging on our backs. Then my new compatriot, Denju Rehn, suddenly turned to me and hugged me with his shocking strength, wishing me all the best. I realized then how much our winter of trials had bound us all together. These men had become the big brothers I had always longed for. After wishing each of them luck, I started out on the road. For some reason I felt like running and yet had no idea where I would run to. All I knew was that the whole mysterious outside world was calling to me and eagerly waiting for me to conquer it.

3 - JOURNEY

The first night on the road was not at all what I had expected. I made my camp off the road and deep enough in the woods that my fire should be hidden from any thugs that might be out there prowling the highways. I sat alone, chewing on a slab of dried beef and wondering if I looked as foolish as I felt. I had set out to find a war art master, yet had I avoided every person I saw coming toward me. My stomach cramped up with the salty meat because I had not stopped to eat all day. I had not wanted any of the others to catch up with me. I guess I felt if they got ahead of me then they might get an apprenticeship with the best master before I found him. I thought about that, then wondered how I would know him if I found him. It was important that I find the best master in all the empire. I had to be the one to return with the best fighting system and win the contest next spring. I thought to ask the people of the first village I came to. But what would they know? Any more than my people knew? Probably not, and their advice might just be a lot of uninformed bluster. I remembered my mother once telling me that deeds build greater monuments than words do.

I prayed that the answer would come to me in a dream. And I thought that it came in a nightmare that very night. I dreamed of a terrible thug catching me on the road. I thought he would pass a poor peasant boy up without taking notice, but he blocked my path. When he demanded money, I looked down to pat my dusty rags and tell him I was only a penniless wanderer. Unfortunately as dreams go, I was dressed in rich brocade and silks. He beat me severely and I woke up just before I would have died in my dream.

The coals of my tiny fire glowed a sullen red in the darkness. The terror of the dream lingered and it seemed the trees were reaching down toward me with rugged wooden hands. "Deeds build greater monuments than words," I whispered in the darkness. "There is no talking a thug out of his spoils." The thug in my dream was a war artist. I could tell by the way he bashed me around with his fists and feet. Suddenly I understood. I had a plan so clever and perfect that it must have come to me through the dream, "A dream sent down from Heaven!" I said aloud. I believed I was given the plan so that I would surely be the victor in the spring contest. It was simple. I would pick fights with those who claimed to be trained in the war arts. Those who beat me the most convincingly would be able to tell me who their teachers were. This way I could find the best master in all the empire. I would not only be the champion of Sanjurra, but my name would be famous throughout Gurin and the surrounding provinces.

13

Warriors, generals and wise men would come to me from afar for advice in all matters of war.

I was overconfident in my predictions of my future grandeur, as one might expect a young farm boy to be. I did follow the plan I devised that night, and I could not have been more sure that it would work, even if a bit painfully. I passed through several villages without finding any who claimed to have studied the war arts. Fortunately some of them told me of a large city to the north. I had never seen a large city and their descriptions seemed both impossible and exciting. In time I came to the city of Jangtoh, and it did not take me long to find some skilled fighters.

At the southern gate of Jangtoh I saw some very tough-looking teenagers. Several of them bore nasty scars and the normal-looking people shied away from them. I walked up to them directly, but they did not seem to notice me or care if they did notice.

"Are you trained in fighting arts?" I asked the toughest looking of them.

Abruptly one of them shoved me from the side and slowly growled, "Would you like training in the dying arts?"

His Jangtoh accent was only slightly difficult for me to understand, but I had never heard an accent before. At the time, I thought he had a speech impediment or was slow in the head.

"Are you slow?" I asked him before thinking about it.

He kicked me in the chest. The funny thing was that I thought his kick was slow. I almost threw my hands out in front fast enough to thwart it. Almost. I hit the dust and rolled over backwards. Before I could stand up, blows rained down on my head, back and shoulders. I could not tell who was doing what. All I knew was that I wanted to get away from them, but I could not get up on my feet to run. Finding a great master was suddenly the last thing on my mind. I pushed against the dusty road of Jangtoh's southern gate with my hands as my blood dripped onto the ground between them. Then the sun seemed to grow dark as my head was battered back and forth. I felt sick. Suddenly I heard something like a hard stick breaking. A terrible scream cut through the darkness and, at first, I thought it was I who had screamed. A body thumped hard to the ground and a young voice groaned in pain. I listened to several slapping sounds as light returned to my eyes. A young man swung his arm like a sword to fell the last of the teenagers with a blow to the neck. I stood up shaky and weak; unable to speak the gratitude I felt.

The stranger grabbed me by the collar of my tunic just as my knees buckled and wavered. He looked at me like I had curled horns on my head

14

and asked, "Are you slow? Those are White Lotus thugs! Now, you've thrown me into their fire. Fool kid! Let's get away from here. This is their territory." He held me by the shoulders of my tunic and rushed me along the amazing streets and alleys of Jangtoh. Eventually I regained the steadiness of my legs and an ache rose up into my head. I could taste blood running from my nose into the back of my throat and mouth. Wiping it from my face, I sniffed the blood up into my nose.

Without slowing his pace, he said, "Don't breathe through your nose. Pinch your nostrils together and don't let go." I kept thinking we would reach the other side of the city and run into the forest. But Jangtoh went on and on. My throat was dry and sore by the time I found myself sitting in a cool dimly-lit room.

The stranger spoke to one of several other young men who were sitting on the floor in the room with us. "Get him some water, please. This wild bumpkin almost got himself planted by the Lotus. And see if Master is here," he called after the man as he left. Then he started to laugh. He laughed so heartily that his friends joined him and I would have laughed too if my head had not been hurting so much. Besides I was afraid to laugh in front of these strangers with my nose pinched between my fingers.

Still laughing, the stranger turned to me and said, "I'm Spear Fist. Who, or what, are you and where did you come from?" Spear Fist's friends inspected his clothes, face and hands.

"I'm Chu Jeng, a farmer's son from Sanjurra village," I said with my nose still pinched shut.

"Where?" a young man asked, rising from the floor with a wide smile and wider eyes. "I've never heard of that village."

The man Spear Fist sent for water returned to the room with two large mugs. He handed one to me and one to Spear Fist. "Master's at the herb market. What is this all about?" he asked, gesturing toward me.

"White Lotus," Spear Fist replied. "Four of them downed. Two planted, I think. This is the best they could do," he said as he pulled down the left side of his tunic to reveal a large bruise already forming on his shoulder.

One of the strangers sucked air through his teeth and said, "You're lucky that was off your deadly band!"

I drank noisily from the mug and all heads turned toward me. Letting go of my nose, I found that the bleeding had stopped. The strangers just stared with polite smiles. I supposed it was time to tell my story. I jumped around clumsily from event to event, but they listened politely.

When I had finished my story, Spear Fist squatted down in front of me

15

and said, "That is the silliest plan I have ever heard. You're not going to find a good teacher that way. You're just going to get killed."

"But it is a divine plan sent to me in a dream," I reminded him.

He only shook his head and said, "You're a skinny little kid who don't look like a threat to anyone. I suppose if you fight with honorable people, you won't be in much danger. But you're a farmer and don't know who to avoid in this city. The White Lotus dogs you ran into wouldn't care if you were a baby! They would be as happy to squash you under their heels as ignore you."

"I believe that," I said. "But I must find the best war art master in all of the empire."

One of the strangers failed to stifle a chuckle. Then he stood up and said, "I have never seen anything like this kid. Anyone this unique can't be left to die on the ugly streets of Jangtoh. Let's give him a rapid course in street work and set him on his way."

Another man nodded and said, "It'll be fascinating. His accent alone is an entertainment. Furthermore, it'll be interesting to see what sprouts from the seed we plant in this country plot, if ever we come to see it."

Three days I stayed with Spear Fist and the men of the Bright Moon Society. I never learned their true names, but heard only their society names like Jade Hand, Whirling Wing, Thunder Foot and Tiger Claws. They told me that the White Lotus was a ruthless criminal gang of southern Jangtoh to be avoided at all costs. The Bright Moon Society was a benevolent neighborhood defense league at war with the Lotus. I believed in their benevolence; for they always acted with honor and kindness toward me. They nursed my wounds and taught me what I needed to know. At the end of my stay, they escorted me far from the White Lotus area of influence. Then they left me at the doorstep of what they said was the best war school in Jangtoh, after their own, of course.

Before leaving, Spear Fist clasped my arm and said, "If you must go on with your doubtful plan, don't insult their Master by asking to fight with him. For Heaven's gain, kid, be careful and remember all we taught you."

I fought with one of the students of the school. He tried to warn me off, but I would not relent. Spear Fist was right. The war artist did not hurt me like the Lotus thugs did. He just kept saying, "Go away, kid!" and knocked me down repeatedly. I noticed his legs were bent strongly outward at the knees while he fought. He did not budge at all when I tried to push him down. I was impressed with his skills, but decided I could not make a judgment without first fighting with other artists. I talked with him afterward and asked him about other war artists. He said I was deranged and told me little of what I wanted to know despite my persistence.

I fought a lot in Jangtoh, then traveled on to other cities. I fought whenever I could and was careful to choose kindly-looking opponents who were supposed to be renowned war artists. I fought and fought and fought. Sometimes I had to wait several days for my bruises and lumps to heal before fighting again. I usually ran, rather than walked, from city to city. Each night I would compare the fighters I had faced. In time, I began to see that the best fighters did certain things alike. The heavily bent legs, sideways stances and high/low guards seemed to work best. I tried imitating them when I was alone, but it did me little good. No combatant ever mistook me for a trained war artist. During my travels, I often heard of a certain man, who most experts regarded as one of the very best fighters in the empire. His name was Draka Von. I was warned not to approach him, though. I was told that he had a bad temper and once killed more than a hundred men in a single fight.

I had to find Draka Von at all costs!

Nearly three months had passed since I left Sanjurra and my parents. Three months of walking, fighting and running had turned my legs to steel and my thoughts to desperation. I was thinking I would never find this Draka Von. Then I saw a man who perfectly fit his description in the crowded market circle of a small village just east of Paigen, capitol of the empire. I instantly knew it had to be the famous Draka. I stood right in front of him, and he turned toward a dried fish stand as if he had not seen me. I tried again to block his path and again he smoothly veered off without seeming to notice. Then I jumped in front of him and growled with my fists clenched up toward him. A man chuckled behind me and Draka Von looked directly into my eyes. I did not see a cruel man with a bad temper. Instead I saw a deeply purposeful blank look that seemed somehow animal and yet extremely intelligent. I took a couple of steps back and fell to my back over a coil of rope. General laughter broke out and Draka Von began to drift away through the crowd. He was heading for the road out of town. I scrambled to my feet and ran after him.

Catching up to him just outside of the market circle, I said, "Draka Von, I have been searching for you for three months."

He turned to me and said, "You're the lunatic farm boy who travels throughout the empire looking for a beating wherever he can find one."

I stood there and stared with my mouth agape.

He resumed walking and said, "Your quest is odd enough to be told in taverns and market places throughout the region."

"You know my whole story?" I asked.

"No. Just that you fight often and don't seem to learn anything from it. I don't know, nor do I care, why you do it. Just leave me out of it."

"But I have to," I insisted.

"Go away," he warned.

Mustering all the courage and manly voice I could, I said, "Draka Von, Prepare to fight!"

"No," he said. He refused to even look at me as he walked toward the edge of town.

"If you will not fight me, then I will attack you!" I rushed him and threw the best attack I could muster.

He instantly broke into a dead run. His long legs carried him quickly out of my reach, but not out of my sight. I ran after him for miles. At last he tired and slowed to a weary walk, and I caught up to him.

Just before I reached him, he turned toward me and said, "No!" between panting breaths.

"I have to! I have to know if you are the best fighter in the empire."

"Your quest is foolish," he said without a hint of emotion. "There is no best fighter in the empire or even in the region. Your way of going about your search is equally foolish. A fight is not a game. People die that way."

Ignoring his admonitions, I put up my fists and took a wild swing at his head. He ducked and ran again. I chased and he gave up after a mile or so. One thing was for sure; I was a better runner than he was. He turned his blank stare on me again, but I did not cringe from him. I stood my ground with fists raised and let out the scariest growl I could. I lunged at him and he sidestepped for me to crash to the ground. My body raised a large puff of dust when it flopped onto the dirt and he began to run. I jumped to my feet and ran after him. He tired quickly and turned to face me as I put up my fists.

"Leave me alone!" he shouted.

I kicked at him and he avoided the kick without having to block it. He squirmed his way out of a punch, another kick and several more punches without contact. I tried to get a hold of his wrist and he wormed away from me.

"I'm losing my patience with you, kid!" He ran a few steps and must have realized again that running away was futile. He stomped his foot and shouted, "Stop it!" Then he leaped into a fighting stance.

It was the most formidable looking stance I had seen in thirty-three fights. I inched forward cautiously, then punched at his belly as fast as I could. He swept my arm out of the way with his hand and I cried out in pain and shock. It felt as if an iron bar had crashed through my wrist. I attacked him again and he left me sprawling in the dust, unharmed but in pain. I got up and made a war face at him. Then he smashed my next kick out of the way and struck me lightly in the back. I flew forward and crashed into the dust once more. When I stood up, he was running again. I caught him easily and the fight resumed. We fought on and on that day. I never landed a blow on him. I never even came close. Draka Von tossed me around like a wet tunic or simply smashed my arms and legs painfully off course. It ended when he somehow threw me into the air and brought my spine down on his knee. I knew instantly that if he had not slowed my fall with his arms, my back would have been broken.

I slid off his knee and knelt with my forehead pressed to the ground. "You are the teacher I have searched for, Draka Von. I will be a faithful and hard-working student. I will never give up or be lazy about anything you have me do. I promise."

"I have no doubt of that! But I don't teach," he panted.

I raised my head and said, "Please teach me, Master. I am no bully or thief. My village sent me to learn a fighting system to defend them from bandits."

"A child? Are all the adults in your village as nuts as you?"

"Others were sent. Nineteen others. All older than I."

"Then go home. Let the older ones do what they should."

"Teach me," I insisted.

Draka Von looked anxiously down the road as if about to run again. "I'm not qualified to teach, boy. Leave me in peace."

I would have none of it. We went on arguing for hours as I followed him home. He warned me sternly not to pass through his gate. By then he was very angry. I waited outside. Early the next morning he found me sleeping in front of his front gate. He tried to sneak back in, but I awoke and asked again to be his disciple. He made a weary face and retreated back inside. I waited and heard his back gate click shut ever so quietly. I caught him running through the woods and followed him all that day. He wearied of the contest but would not relent to teach me, even after three more days had passed. In the end he told me of his teacher as we approached his gate just before nightfall.

"Master Kanoh will probably come down and kill me for this, but I will send you to him. My only other choices are to die just for some rest or kill you just for relief from your relentless nagging. If there is a best fighter in all the empire, it would be Master Kanoh. I was his first student and his last student. You can go and ask him to teach you, but he will not. I will tell you where to find him only if you promise never to bother me again."

"I promise I will never pester you again if you send me to him."

"Good!" Draka Von said, and he looked as if he would cry with relief. "Come in and eat with me. On my oath, kid, you can work up a man's appetite! When we have supped, I will tell you how to behave with the Master. Try the foolishness you tried with me and he will not even talk to you. Then what? Huh? Where will you go then?"

When Draka Von served the evening meal, I thought I might have been in Heaven. I had not enjoyed a home-cooked meal since I left Sanjurra and Draka was an excellent cook. He served potatoes fried in spiced butter, breaded chicken in a tangy red sauce and stir-fried vegetables. What a feast! I slept well that night and set into my mind all the advice he had given me. The next morning I left a very happy Draka Von behind and started out on what he said would be a three-week journey. I ran most of the way and rested as little as possible. I reached the master's secluded mountain cottage in only a week and a half.

4 - STUDY

Draka Von's directions were clear, but physically difficult to follow. He had told me that Master Kanoh lived where no man would bother him; where no man was likely to find him. I had to climb up craggy mountain paths that seemed to defy the logic that would guide a normal traveler. The special marks Draka told me about were difficult to find, but not impossible. Eventually I came to a plateau of thick, dark forest. The trees were crowded together as if huddled in fear. I struggled to walk straight west from the top end of the rocky path as Draka Von had instructed me. The trees wanted desperately to thwart my straight line of travel. They blocked out most of the weak evening sunlight that filtered its way through the clouds and made it difficult for me to sense direction. The air up there was wet, cool and thin. It seemed almost useless to my lungs. Just when I would have given myself up for lost, I broke into a grassy clearing. At the other side of the glade, a thin ribbon of water cascaded down a towering face of gray stone. The water dissolved into a light mist before disappearing into a rich green mass of tangled growth near a crystal pool. Against the face of the cliff, at the edge of the pool, stood a cottage of stone with a high peaked roof of slate shingles. A large circle of smooth raked sand stood about fifty feet in front of the cottage. The sand was lined with a mortared wall of stones, perhaps a foot high. At the edge of the sand nearest the cottage, an arch of dark stone with a wooden gate inside and no wall outside stood high and foreboding. A small gong and clapper hung near the latch. Draka said the Master's dwelling was beautiful, but I had not expected it to be so stunning in its rustic charm. Despite the dwelling, circle of sand and gate, I felt as if I were the first person ever to set foot in the glade. Following my feelings, I removed my sandals and walked toward the cottage. I crossed the sand to the gate and took the clapper in my hand. I stood there rehearsing what I would say to the Master, when suddenly D felt a gentle tapping on my shoulder.

I turned to see a very old man with a wisp of a white mustache and a scanty fringe of white hair. He looked weak and frail, but his eyes were filled with the power of a tiger.

"I know," he said as I opened my mouth to speak my name. "You are the fighting farmer boy. Draka must have told you I do not teach." He walked around me and examined me in silence as I nervously fumbled through my traveling bundle for my letters of introduction. "If you were any thinner or more bedraggled I would have thought you a ghost of the fighting farm boy come to haunt me."

21

I struggled to keep my voice from shaking as I said, "I have letters of introduction from my village Elders."

Master Kanoh took the letters from me and I kept silent as he read. At length he said, "Your Elders know nothing."

I was shocked that even one as ancient as he would be so disrespectful to the Elders. "Teach me, Master, you are my only hope at this late time. The others are doubtless all accomplished war artists by now."

He laughed quietly. "Stand here and do not move. I'll be back after I consider your request." Then he opened the strange gate and walked through it to his cottage.

I watched the shadows grow long. I did not move. The shadow of the forest crept halfway up the face of the rock and then faded into darkness, and I did not move. Stars began to peek through the dispersing clouds and my legs cramped, but I did not move. Morning broke on my weariness and I thought surely the Master would come out. The noon sun hammered down upon me and my stomach growled in desperate hunger. Still I did not move. When the evening sun began to fall behind me, I heard the strange, fenceless gate unlatching in front of me. Master Kanoh stepped through and his face took on a look of shock. I did not move or speak a word. I made my face as impassive as I could. He walked around me in silence. He plucked at my tunic and the day's dust fell from its folds. He stopped and looked at the urine-washed sand in front of me. He stooped to see where my feet had slowly dug themselves deep into the sand during my long wait.

At last he stood and nodded slowly with his eyebrows raised. "Only one before you has ever shown such patience and perseverance. I truly thought you would be gone by now." When he smiled, I knew he had accepted me as his student. I could have jumped in the air and screamed for joy. Then his face grew stern. "I practice in this circle of sand. Now you have used it for a latrine! I will get you a shovel and bucket. Remove this soiled sand and throw it off my mountain!" Then he walked away muttering, "Absurd farmers think all soil has to be fertile!"

He returned with a small spade and a wooden bucket. I removed the sand as fast as I could and ran through the forest to throw it over the precipice that lined his secluded plateau. When I returned, the Master had a cold meal prepared for us. I restrained my ravening hunger to eat with all the manners I could muster. After the meal, grogginess hit me like a falling rock. The Master stared at me sitting on his stone floor and struggling to stay awake.

Desperation driving me toward impoliteness, I asked, "May I sleep,

Sir."

"Sleep," he said quietly. Before I could ask where I should sleep, I fell over and began dreaming.

Master Kanoh woke me before sunrise the next morning in the very spot where I had fallen asleep. "Get up if you plan to learn anything," he said, standing over me with a candle giving off a weak, warm light.

"Did you put this pillow under my head?" I asked groggily.

He only grunted and shook his head in response. "Come, child," he said as he walked away. He blew the candle out as he opened the door to step outside. A thin jagged line of silver and orange light painted the clouds near the bit of the southeastern horizon I could see around the towering cliff. Master stripped off his robes and leggings and hung them on a hook near the door. Lifting one of two wooden buckets from the stone steps, he poured half of it over his head. I removed my grimy, dusty rags and did the same, setting my nearly empty money belt aside. The bucket was heavy and the water shockingly cold. I reeled and almost dropped the bucket; spilling the rest of it.

"Get more water from the pool," Master growled.

When I returned with the heavy buckets, my old clothes were on fire. The smoke smelled foul. Master was just putting his robes and a fresh pair of leggings back on. I scrubbed myself as instructed while he disappeared into the house. I dressed in a new set of robes and leggings he brought out for me.

"I altered those myself. Do everything myself. Ships are supported by water, that's why the water can overturn them. You remember that, boy." Throughout my stay with him, Master proved himself to be a veritable fountain of proverbs. He usually punctuated them with a command that I remember them. Other times he would describe a situation which called for a proverb I had heard before. If I did not respond quickly enough, he would ask me why I didn't remember things I was told to remember. I followed him into the woods along a path I could barely detect. We came to a lush garden and he instructed me very sternly and thoroughly as to what plants to tend and how. "Hard work is, always has been and ever will be the only path to success," he barked at me. After several hours of gardening, I wondered if he wanted me to think the weeding was some sort of war art training. At last he said, "Let us have some breakfast." We jogged back to the cottage and ate some cheese and some cold rice and drank hot aromatic tea. When we had finished, Master Kanoh washed our dishes and walked me out to the smooth circle of sand. I thought I had come to the real training at last! I could hardly contain my excitement.

"Have you ever ridden a horse, farm boy?"

"No, sir. My family is poor."

"Have you seen anyone ride a horse?" he said with a look of impatience.

"Yes, Sir."

"Good. Stand with your legs bent as if you were riding on a horse's back and place your fists at your sides like this." He demonstrated how he wanted me to put my hands.

I spread my legs apart and bent my knees outward as if I were on a horse's back. It reminded me of the stances used by those I had fought on my journey.

Master Kanoh suddenly lunged toward me from the front, but did not touch me. I tilted backward, unsuccessfully flailed my arms for balance and fell on my seat. Master laughed and said, "Get up and try it again. This time aim your toes forward. You must begin thinking about angles, leverage and support. You pointed your toes out as if standing on a fence rail. That reduced your angle of support. This is a square horse stance. Everything you would do improperly sitting on a horse is improper for this stance. There are no horses here on Lungshan, but you will learn to ride. Now make your feet parallel. Good. Now bend your knees farther outward. The first reason I will tell you for properly bent knees is that it protects them from getting bent the wrong way." Then he kicked me harshly in the knee from the side. My leg flexed painlessly inward with the blow. "That would have rendered you a cripple for the rest of your life if your knee were not properly bent. Remember that, boy! Now think about what I've told you and don't move from that stance. Don't move at all! I'll be back." Then he walked into the forest.

I was proud that I resisted the kick of a real war art master. I basked in the glory of that success and reveled in the iron strength of my legs. All the walking and running I had done over the last three and a half months had given me powerful legs that were already impressing my new Master. The smile began to fade from my face as a burning sensation started up in my legs. Soon they began to shake. After a while, I wanted desperately to stand up and relax my legs, but Master said not to move and I felt sure he was secretly watching me from the forest. So I stood there shaking and sweating, my feet quivering themselves down into the deep cool sand. I began to think that I had the weakest legs in the world. Then I saw Master Kanoh walking from the forest toward his cottage.

"Endurance, my boy. It's the key to success," he called back to me without looking to see how I was suffering. "He who tires in battle dies in that same battle. Remember that, boy!" The door slammed behind him and I thought I would fall down any moment. He eventually came out, but I don't know how long after he had gone in. My robes and leggings were soaked with sweat. I was on the verge of crying with the pain, but I refused to let out even a small groan.

"Why are you sweating?" he asked. "It's not hot out here!" He looked up toward the sun as if to emphasize his statement. "I love this weather." Then he looked at me shaking desperately. "What is wrong with you? Get out of that stance and run around the circle. Get some blood flowing in those legs and then let's get to work."

When I finished stumbling my way around the circle, he called me to follow him into the forest. We walked for about a half a mile and came to a grove of sapling pines. "Cut six of these down, strip their branches off and haul them back to my cottage." He looked at the incredulous look on my face and said, "You don't expect me to build your hut, do you? I can't spend every night listening to you snore in my dining room either." He walked off and left me in the grove alone.

"I don't snore," I whispered when I though he was far enough away. Then I began to wonder if, perhaps, I really did snore and only failed to know it because I was sleeping when I did it. I found a war axe leaning up against one of the saplings and went to work. I cut the straightest six of the trees and finished hauling them back to the cottage just before nightfall.

I stood sweating and panting over the last log when Master called me in for the evening meal. I ate as if starved near to death.

Master wiped his mouth after finishing and said, "Nothing like good, hard, honest work to butter the bread and sauce the meat. Not true, farm boy?"

"Yes, Sir," I replied.

"It's unfortunate that you didn't get to do much practicing today. Won't tomorrow, either. We will have to build your hut then, near the side of my cottage. For now, let's do what little practice we can." I followed him out to the circle of sand and we did just the thing I dreaded most. We stood facing each other in square horse stances. We stood there without a word. I shook and sweated while he seemed as comfortable as if reclining in bed. After an interminably painful time, he led me in a run around the circle and set up a crude bed for me in his dining room.

I awoke the next day to the same routine. A splash bath of icy water, gardening, breakfast and then he had me stand in a horse stance until I thought my legs would bleed fire. We nearly finished my little hut and then we ate the evening meal. More horse stance followed and then I collapsed in bed. The next day was the same. While standing in the horse stance, I figured he would get started on the real war art training after my hut was finished. After my usual stumbling run around the sand pit, which Master always raked during the night, he took me on a hike through the forest. We reached the edge of the lofty plateau and he showed me a great pile of bundled long grass.

"Thatch to finish your hut," he said pointing at the bundles.

"Where did you get these?" I asked. Nowhere on his plateau had I seen anything like the long coarse grass bundled before me and stacked higher than my head.

"Down there," he said, pointing toward a grassy table nearly four-hundred feet below. I crept to the edge of the rocks and peered over the precipice. I could see no safe way up or down. I turned to see him disappearing into the forest with a bundle on his back.

Catching up to him with my own bundle, I said, "Master, you climbed all the way down there and then up with these heavy, clumsy bundles on your back? You could have been killed!"

"I had to risk it to get some peace from your snoring," he said without looking back.

We thatched the roof of my hut and I ground a powder of lime with two large flat rocks. He said he quarried and fired the lime from a deposit on the western side of his mountain. He had me apply a stucco of lime paste to the mud-plastered lattice walls while he stood by grousing and groaning about my workmanship. In the end he grunted his reluctant approval and said that when I was gone he could use the hut for a storage shed. He helped me to fit a very fine woven lattice of slivered wood to the single small window that faced east. Then he peg-hinged rain shutters to the outside.

The next day's routine changed only in that we ate three meals instead of two and I stood in a horse stance three grueling times instead of twice. Each time I stood in the terrible horse stance a little bit longer. The burning pain was beginning to take longer to come to me. I wanted to say something about the redundant practice and lack of teaching. Then I remembered Draka Von's stern warnings that any complaint, no matter how small, would get me immediately dismissed.

The routine continued on the same way for more than a month. I was sure the Master could see that I was about to burst with frustration. I had already shown him that I could stand in a horse stance for nearly half a day, but he continued on with it. I stood in the stance and listened to him lecture about the merits of the horse stance. He told me hundreds of war stories and tales of the great war artists of history like the story of Ken Gar, old Iron Legs.

Ken Gar, he told me, was a famous bear style war art master from the Ganju Mountains. After twenty-five years of hard, faithful study, Ken Gar made his way throughout the Empire demonstrating his powerful stance. He would wager money that, even with blows from heavy sticks, the locals could not disturb his powerful horse stance. Through such wagering, he made a good living and never lost a single bet on his praiseworthy stance. Then one day Ken Gar bet a farmer that his mule could not kick his legs out of proper stance. The whole village gathered and very few bets were on Ken Gar. But, to everyone's surprise, Ken Gar's powerful stance resisted every kick of the mule. The crowd cheered the master and praised him resoundingly. He even cheered for himself and turned to face the crowd with his arms stretched up in triumph. That's when the mule kicked him in the back and killed him.

Some of the stories were impossible to believe; others were sad, confusing or even comical. Through his stories I learned that the original war arts were devised by observing the fighting movements of animals and imitating them. "Animals are the true war art masters," he told me. All the stories ended with some sort of proverbial lesson for me and the inevitable, "Now you remember that, boy!" I felt stifled in the training and frustrated beyond my capacity to hold my complaints back any longer.

One morning Master woke me with a loud shout instead of his usual, "Get up if you plan to learn anything." I clambered halfway to my feet and staggered into the wall of my hut before falling back to the floor in utter confusion. Master stood at the door laughing and said, "Your lack of effort has stifled my renowned ability to train he who would excel in the war arts. It is time to change strategies." I could have screamed, but I kept my mouth clamped shut. I had been trying as hard as I could to please him and felt that he should have recognized my efforts.

I followed him into the forest and we walked straight past the garden. Eventually we came to a wooden rack suspended under the branch of a great tree by a single heavy rope that looped down to the branch of another tree. The rack was octagonal in shape and about ten feet from side to side. It had hundreds of identical sharp spikes sticking straight down from its underside. I looked at the ground beneath the rack and saw that it was heavily scuffed with foot prints.

"Get under the rack," Master said. I walked onto the scuffed ground and looked up at the threatening spikes in the dim light of morning. Master Kanoh began lowering the rack by giving it more rope from the small tree where it was tied off. He cleared his throat and said, "You better get into a horse stance, boy. It's coming down." I lowered myself into the all-too-familiar stance. "Much lower, boy. Get so low that your thighs are parallel with the ground. Yes. Just like that. That is called a flat horse. It isn't used for fighting, but it is good for strengthening the legs. A fight should never be conducted at the limit of your skills and powers. That's why we do things like the flat horse. Make fighting skills far more difficult in training than they will ever be on the street and you will do well when it comes to the street. Something to think about, boy. Now, the rack will convince you not to relieve your legs by rising up." With that he walked away toward his garden.

He returned after what seemed to me to be an eternity in hell. It must have been obvious to him that I was suffering. Tears streamed down my cheeks along with the sweat. "Relieve one of your legs like this," he said, forming what I would later come to know as a flat bow and arrow stance. It was called bow and arrow stance because the forward leg was bent like a bow and the rear leg was locked into the ground and held straight like an arrow. Master usually referred to it as a bow stance. While under the rack, one could only use flat stances, which were deeper versions of the normal fighting stances. He had me switch from the bow and arrow stance to the fighting cat stance to the twist stance and back to the horse. I learned the fighting horse stance to replace the square horse, which was only used for practice. I even learned that my arms and shoulders could burn like my legs as I held them in a proper guard for hours at a time. Master was even thoughtful enough to hand me rocks to hold in my hands for the building of upper body strength and endurance.

During the month I trained under the rack, I learned to maneuver and my legs became knotted cords of rock-hard muscle that could take almost anything. Though I could see my stance progressing in strength and maneuverability, I was growing very frustrated that he was not teaching me any fighting skills. I could not rid myself of the fear that I would be the only one of the twenty to return home without a fighting system.

One morning as the sun rose, Master Kanoh had me stand in the center of the sand circle in a normal fighting horse. I was allowed to leave my stance only to run off to relieve myself of waste then run back to the sand and resume the horse. I took my meals standing in a horse stance and meditated upon Master's stories while standing in the horse. When I noticed the sun had set I also noticed that I had not sweated a drop and my legs had not begun to shake. Though thrilled at my success, I was frightened that this was to be a new month-long phase in my training without any war art study.

I could see that his training would have been helpful if I had fifty years to train with him. Unfortunately, I had only five and a half months left to train with him and one month to make the journey home. That night the thought that I had failed in my quest hit me, and my heart ached at the shame I would bring upon my parents. I lay in my hut and wept in bitter silence. There was no possibility that I could find another great master who would train me fast enough. I cursed myself for the foolish plan I had followed. Even if I had found a poor war artist and trained with him, it would have been more productive. In my bitterness, though, I could not bring myself to curse the old man. He had always spoken harshly to me and firmly denied caring the least for me, but I knew he loved me. He poured his best teaching into me, but his best teaching was too slow for my needs. No, I could not blame him. The failure was mine; a failure of my own stupid pride that could only result in the embarrassment that comes as the just reward for pride. I decided tell Master Kanoh the next day that I must leave early for my home in shameful failure.

5 - APPRENTICESHIP

Master woke me the next morning by throwing a bucket of ice cold water on me. I leapt up into a fighting horse stance without thinking or knowing what was happening.

"Get that forward guard closer to your shoulder, before I rip it off!" he growled. Then in a more fatherly tone, "Set your hut in order, immediately. I want to test your progress." With that, he walked away as I dripped onto the earthen floor of my little home. I wiped my face and wished myself a happy fourteenth birthday before setting about cleaning my hut.

Master Kanoh returned with a cloth-covered basket. He set the basket on the floor of my freshly-cleaned hut and then sat down on the floor. He motioned for me to sit and I dropped to the floor, wondering what he had in store for me. I also wondered how I would be able to tell him I had to leave for home.

"Chu Jeng, one who walks the warrior's path becomes sensitive to minute movements of the body. I am sensitive not only to the movements of my body, but also sensitive to yours. I am likewise sensitive to movements of the mind and emotions. You want to leave. You feel that your learning is too slow. That is only because you don't understand what's happening to you here." He reached into the basket and pulled an expensive looking inkwell and a fine set of brass quills from beneath the cloth cover. He also set out a chamber pot, a heavy stack of blank paper, candles and a large brass lock. "You may leave as you wish, but I ask you to spend just a few more days here with me. I will lock you in this hut and bring you food and water every day. I will empty and clean your chamber pot and see that you have all that you need. I challenge you to write all that you know about the fighting horse stance on this paper. When you have correctly answered my question and asked the right question, then you will be more able to wisely choose the rest of your path."

I knew somehow that his offer was of the utmost importance to the rest of my life, perhaps even to my final destiny. I felt my head nodding in agreement and he left without a word. I heard him attach the lock to the outer latch of my door. I picked up the top sheet of paper and stared at its blankness in the dim morning light that reached through my only window. Even the days were cool by then and I drew my thin woolen blanket around my shoulders as I sat and thought. After a while, I figured a full description of the horse stance should only take me a couple of hours. I began writing. I soon filled up several sheets and felt rather satisfied with my success. I fell back on my bed to relax. But, somehow I could not relax at all. I felt restless and wanted to flex my legs or do something. I almost felt like I wanted to stand in a horse stance! I laughed out loud in my hut with the sun streaming in on the papers I had written. Then I realized that I had described the horse stance without telling about what the stance does, both offensively and defensively. I had heard the countless stories Master Kanoh told me about the horse stance and its uses in combat. There was much more to tell than I had written. I picked up the papers and began to write again.

Soon my legs began to cramp. My shoulders ached and I wanted to move and flex my idle muscles. I wrote in between the aches and cramps, but the restlessness did not go away. Master brought me some breakfast and replaced the chamber pot. He glanced down at the stack of papers I had written and smiled with raised eyebrows. Several times I thought surely I had written all there was to know about the horse stance. Then a new thought would come to me and I would pick up a quill and the ink would start flowing again. I wrote through lunch and dinner and more painful cramps. Master Kanoh returned with the setting of the sun and read my papers in silence by candlelight.

When he finished reading he asked, "Is that all there is to know about the fighting horse stance?"

I answered, "I think so, Sir."

He grunted with disgust and asked, "What is your question?"

"Can I come out now?" I asked, not knowing what else to ask, and feeling like a fool as soon as the words escaped my lips.

"Oh! For Heaven's gain!" he said with a look of sheer disappointment. He left and locked the door.

The next day I woke up by myself and started to write. I tried to think of what I had missed before. "What more could I possibly write?" I asked myself. My muscles began to ache and alternate between thirsting for exercise and cramping. Somehow I filled several more pages with what I thought was pretty good material. Then after breakfast I tried hard to think of a good answer and question for Master Kanoh. I thought hard and long as I wrote throughout the day and my answer and question filled him with disappointment at sunset.

The next day was much the same as was the next and the next. On the sixth day, though, My legs cramped less and ached less for exercise. It was not until the ninth day that I realized my muscles were losing their steel and vigor. I began to feel desperate, afraid and frustrated with my apparent lack of progress. Then on the sunset of my eleventh day of writing, I came to understand. I sat on my bed looking at the bare spot where my clean papers had been. There in the nothingness of that space was the answer. When Master Kanoh opened the door, I think he saw the understanding in my eyes. He did not even bother to look at the last few pages I had written.

"Is that all there is to know about the horse stance?" he asked slowly, perhaps even hopefully.

"No, Master Kanoh. No single lifetime is long enough to understand all there is to know in the horse stance."

He nodded his head for a long time with his eyes squinted as if deep in thought. "Do you have a question for me, young man?"

I hoped my question was the right one. I felt in my heart that it was the only honest thing I could ask at that time. "Is there enough paper in the world that an adequate description of the horse stance could be written?"

I think he looked at me as a man for the first time then. Never again did he refer to me as a boy. He squeezed my shoulder with his hand and said, "Sleep, my young apprentice. We will start a fast and difficult path tomorrow."

He kept his promise so well that I almost regretted it. That next day Master and I stretched our muscles for two hours before beginning his training routine. I did fifteen-thousand punches in the air and five-hundred against sand bags that day. Most of the time I stood in a horse stance. Master cooked for me and tended to my every need as if I were his prize war horse in training. He talked of honoring my parents and my village Elders while I sweated and perfected my movements. Other times he would tell me war stories. Some times he made me laugh, then pretended to be angry as he scolded me for laughing and failing to take the study seriously. As the days went on, I learned many kinds of blocks, kicks and strikes. We did the hard work of war art training from predawn until far into the darkness of night. Master firmly believed in repetition of basic movements as the path to perfection. He often had me clash my arms against his own in blocking movements. He applied miraculously potent salves to my bruises, contusions and aching muscles. I drank potions for strength, endurance and health. The months flew by and I thought I had become a man that my parents would barely recognize. All my muscles were knotted and sculpted like stone. I could easily touch my chin to the ankle of my straightened leg.

He trained me to break sticks with my hands, elbows, feet, knees, forearms and shins. I held a flat horse under the falling icy mist of the waterfall while holding a particular thought he would give me. Other times he would make me stand in the frigid pool and throw a few thousand punches into the water. One night toward the end of my training he ordered me to start punching the center of the sand pit. I punched it until a large depression had formed beneath me. He said to continue punching it and stomp-kicking it until the hole was deep enough that I could stand in it up to my waist. I slammed that narrow hole down beneath the sand for two days. Occasionally I came to rocks; which Master let me throw out of the hole for him to haul out of the sand circle. Master applied salves to my fists that made the skin of my already deeply calloused knuckles like hardened leather. When the hole was as deep as he had asked, I slept for nearly a day. When I awoke, he fed me and gave me potions and herbal teas to drink. Then he led me to the hole and showed me that he had cleared the two feet of sand away from the hard earth of the hole.

"Get into the hole," he told me.

I clambered in and wondered what outrageous and painful thing he would have me do next. I thought it very peculiar that I was hoping for some insanely difficult challenge. I began to breathe hard in anticipation.

"Place your fists on your ribs and jump straight up out of the hole into a square horse stance with your feet near the edges."

I jumped and barely cleared the hole to land in my stance.

"Now jump back down and do it again. Then repeat the exercise until the east and west sides of the hole are beaten down to the bottom."

It only took me about ten hours to slam the sides of the horse pit down because my feet dragged some of the dirt from the sides down into the pit. Still, I rested and nearly collapsed many times and he had to give me potions to keep me going. I think those ten hours did nearly as much for the strength of my horse stance as all my time under the rack in the forest had done. After that, we continued our work with long grueling days of practicing basic movements. As the weeks wore on, I grew to enjoy the challenge of overcoming whatever difficult task he threw at me. He could not do some of the things my youthful body allowed me to do, but my basic movements were still not nearly as powerful or as perfected as his.

I appreciated his supreme efforts in training me, but as the time neared for me to go home I began to worry again. I had learned many basic movements and hardened my muscles and abilities far beyond anything I had imagined before the quest began; yet I had no direct knowledge of how to apply the basic movements to an actual fight. Every time I imagined some thug attacking me, my mind went blank. I simply did not know what to do in a real fighting situation.

I lingered perhaps a week longer than I should have at Master Kanoh's mountain sanctuary. He drilled me relentlessly until one morning I said, "Master Kanoh, I cannot go home without a fighting system. Please let me stay here with you."

He stared at me for a long time before he made his answer. "Young man of the house of Chu, would you run away from your duty? Whatever superficial shame you fear is far less important than the true shame you would bring to yourself by cheating your Elders and your family. Your father and mother have no other sons to take care of them when they grow old. Would you throw them to loneliness and starvation?"

I felt trapped. Trying to keep my voice from shaking, I said, "I have great respect for your instruction, Master, but I have not learned to fight. I will shame my parents if I return to make a fool of myself in the village tournament next month."

Master Kanoh smiled and said, "Do you think any of the others learned a complete fighting system in a single year or less? Impossible! I lived with my Master for nineteen exhausting years before he named me a master warrior. With the little time we had, I have hardened you like steel in the fire. Go home and conquer, Chu Jeng." He watched me struggle with disbelief for a while then said, "It is more difficult for us men to see our selves as we are than it is for birds to understand the air that lifts them or fish to know the water that bears them. Chu Jeng, I have given you all that you need to prevail in the contest of your village. You will face no accomplished war artists there. If you do not return to them, then you will have to find some other place of refuge. I will be happy if you return to me some day with honor, but I will not assist you in any shameful act of cowardice or disobedience."

I knew it would accomplish nothing for me to argue with him. So I resolved myself to go home. Master returned my money belt to me with more money in it than when I came to him, though he firmly denied contributing. He did openly admit filling my traveling bundle with rations. He even included a potion for me to drink on the morning of the tournament.

The last thing he said to me as I walked toward the forest to leave his plateau was, "The name of the war art you began to study is Iron Fist. Honor our system and let no other style shame us!"

I traveled south and east by a different route, avoiding most of the cities I had come through on my way to Master Kanoh. The robes I wore on my way back attracted several thugs, who tried to rob me out on the open road. I easily outran them all. In fact, I lightly ran most of the way home because I left a little later in the year than I should have. My traveling was shorter and much faster, though, for not having to search for war artists and fight with them. Neither did I have to rest while injuries healed.

All throughout my journey home Master Kanoh's wisdom and admonitions filled my thoughts. To occupy my time, I would repeat as many of his proverbs as I could while running. I counted one-hundred-forty-six of them that I could remember word for word. Many others left their mark on my thinking even though I could not find the exact wording he had used. Each night before sleeping, I would stand in a flat horse stance for about a half-hour while practicing basic arm movements. When I slept, I dreamed of Master Kanoh and his secluded glade on Lungshan Mountain. He had said once that I was only the third person ever to set foot upon his secret plateau. I dreamed that I would one day live on a mountaintop like Master Kanoh and teach the Iron Fist system to my students. When I woke up on the next morning, I realized how foolish my dream was. I could never teach a system I had only started to learn. The realization of my incomplete training haunted me from that morning on until I reached my home three days later.

6 - FESTIVAL

I stepped from the woods and gazed upon the farm house of my fathers only two days before the first day of spring. It was late afternoon and I thought I had never beheld a sight more beautiful; yet the beauty was marred by my dread of impending defeat and shame. Nevertheless, I was almost drunk with the familiar old smells of my father's farm and the spring wildflowers. The bright green of new growth was everywhere and sprinkles of red, purple, and yellow-orange blossoms fought with each other for my attention. My father's fields were bursting with fresh growth. His livestock pen teemed with nanny goats and their frolicking kids. I felt a sudden urge to run to the pen and romp with the playful, round-headed kids and forget the contest that would begin on the day after tomorrow. Then Master Kanoh's words came to me, *Honor is the diamond that scratches every other stone. You remember that, boy!*

"I remember, Master Kanoh," I said aloud, and drew a deep breath before starting toward my house with an odd mixture of doubt and joy. Mother saw me coming across the northern fields before I reached our back door. She ran out to me, crying and laughing at the same time. Some of the manly self-definition I had gained on Master Kanoh's mountain fell away from me at that moment. I rushed to her and hugged her waist. I had somehow forgotten that she was a full head taller than I.

"Jeng! Look at you," she said, breaking away to hold me by the shoulders at arms length. "You've gained a couple of inches I'd say. You're so hard to the touch. Your shoulders are like little rocks!" She looked at my expression and quickly corrected, "No. They're like big rocks." We both laughed and then stood in awkward silence for a moment. "Are you hungry, Jeng? You look starved. There just isn't the slightest bit of fat on you!"

"I am hungry, mom. I've hungered so long for this farm and for you and dad that I..." She hugged me again. Then we walked, arm-in-arm to the rough little farmhouse I had always loved as if it were Heaven. A full year of living out of doors, then in a hut, had made that old house into something like a rich palace in my eyes.

As soon as my father returned from the village, Mother raced to my deceased uncle's farm and told his wife and daughters that I had returned from the quest. Within hours, our little house was filled with our relatives and friends. We feasted as they caught me up on village gossip. I tried to avoid talking about my incomplete training. But there was no way to

37

change the subject when the feasting was through and the men gathered around the glowing embers of the cooking pit. The moon had risen bright in the sky making the landscape look cooler than it was, but the season's heat was in me, both from the happiness of my homecoming and from fears over my incomplete skills.

Individual conversations trailed off one by one, then Father broke the silence by saying, "Jeng, show us farmers your war art."

It was just the demand I had expected and dreaded most. How could I tell them I did not have a war art? The clever objections I had already prepared fell from my mind and I could only say, "It's hard to show, Father," I hoped against reason that they would let the subject drop.

They all began to shout at once, laughing and encouraging me to demonstrate the mysterious warrior skills I had learned. Most of them had never traveled more than twenty miles from the village area. I had traveled the outside world and become a mystery to them. I was a hero of sorts.

"Demonstrate a feat for us, Chu Jeng," Uncle Weng called out loudly. He had become a bit uninhibited with too much drink. "The other men of the quest are performing amazing tricks in the village."

Father took the floor to shut his brother up before his slurred speech could shame him further. "Give us something, Jeng. Isn't there something you can show us?" The others began again to shout their encouragement. I could see no way out of it, so I decided to break a stick for them.

"I can break a stick," I said. The mob was instantly silenced. "Get me a stick, from the forest and I will break it." After a moment of indecision, one of my cousins ran for the forest and the others followed in a chattering mob. Only my father remained by the glowing coals with me.

He poured himself a drink from the keg and said, "You are more a man than I expected would return to me, Jeng. You're strong in body and in spirit. I can see that. I can feel it. When you were much younger, I sometimes feared that you would not grow up strong enough to... well, carry on after me. But now I'm confident and very proud that you came back as you are."

The noisy mob of cousins and uncles returned one-by-one with armloads of sticks of all sizes. They dropped the sticks at my feet and stood back laughing and chattering in subdued tones.

I backed up and said, "Throw them to me. That's what my Master did toward the end of my study." Actually, he threw them *at* me, but I did not want to deal with dangerous projectiles in the moonlight. Father picked up a small stick and cautiously tossed it to me. It was a perfect throw and I cut down through the stick with a right knifehand chop. It snapped loudly in two, the ends spinning toward the ground. The rest of the men and boys scrambled for sticks to throw. It was kind of them to choose the lighter sticks first, but soon sticks as thick as my arms remained. These I had them hold for me to break with my feet or forearms. When the last chunk of wood cracked into two heavy pieces, we threw its ends into the fire along with the rest. They paraded me around on their shoulders and cheered while the fire reached for the sky. My mother, aunts and female cousins clambered outside and joined the cheering. They declared me champion of the Chu clan and swore that I would soon be the champion of the village. I smiled, but knew that fighting was more than just breaking sticks. I had fought more than thirty fights since I left home a year ago. I lost every fight rather miserably.

The Elders decided to hold the spring festival on the day before the first day of spring. They wanted to keep the first day of spring for the village tournament. They called the men of the quest forward to discuss the tournament rules. Twelve of us had returned by noon when the rules were made. Even the discussions of fighting gave me a helpless queasy feeling in the pit of my stomach. The rules came out to be very simple. No weapons could be used in the fighting. Nobody could break anybody's bones or cause permanent injury. A twenty-foot-diameter circle was to be formed on the ground for contestants to fight two at a time. A contestant lost when he was either knocked out of the circle, decided to give up, or was rendered incapable of continuing. Each fight was to start with an introduction of the fighters and a clap of Elder Korenda's hands. Fighters were to be chosen by lot and eliminated until one was left the victor. I walked away from the Rules Committee Meeting with my stomach close to vomiting.

The spring festival opened the next morning with a rousing speech from Elder Korenda. He told us that an age of prosperity and peace was about to dawn on our village and all the surrounding area because of the decision he and his council of elders had made. The people all cheered and slapped the nearest man of the quest on the back. Names of favorite contestants were shouted amid the cheering, mostly by their own relatives. Then names of fighting styles were shouted; like Southern Dragon, Black Tiger, Leopard, White Crane, Whirling Fists and Mountain Long Fist. I should have hollered out the name of Master Kanoh's Iron Fist style, but I just wanted to hide. Soon the kegs were tapped, pies and other baked goods sold and livestock auctioned. The richer farmers of the soil brought out their draft horses and engaged in pulling contests. Women displayed their needle work and cooking skills. The Elders were, of course, the judges of all the cooking contests. I guessed that the true reason they moved the festival was so the tournament would not interfere with their favorite day of the year.

During the festival some of the war artists demonstrated their martial skills. I only watched a few of the demonstrations. Avoiding them did not help me, though. The exaggerated talk that swept through the crowd terrified me even more than the sight of the demonstrations. I wandered the quieter places of the festival and ran into Denju Rehn, the burly potter's son. He flashed a brief unhappy smile.

"Hello, Denju," I said, surprised to see him alone instead of showing off his bear-like strength.

"Hello, Chu. I'm glad to see you back and safe from the quest."

I looked around and asked him, "Why aren't you showing your prowess with the rest of them?"

"Strength isn't everything, Chu. I found that out on the quest." He paused and seemed to struggle with some inner thought. Then he said, quietly, "Chu, I didn't have time to learn a fighting system."

"What did you do for a year?" I asked him, wondering if he never found a teacher and trying to hide the fact that I had no complete system either.

"I studied a mixed tiger and crane war art system. I had a lot of problems though. I tried to rely on my strength too much. Honestly, I just couldn't learn fast enough. Master told me all along that I needed to slow down and relax. I don't know what I am going to do tomorrow. I tell you, Chu, I even thought of not coming home!"

I barely suppressed an urge to laugh out loud. Imagine, the mountainous tower of strength, the pony-carrying friend to anyone in need of a strong back, the rock-muscled Denju Rehn, Denju the rock, cowering in a dark corner! At length, I had to tell him, "I did exactly the same, Denju. My master told me that none of the others could possibly learn a complete fighting system in even five years."

Suddenly Denju straightened up as if a weight were lifted from his shoulders. "I thought I was the only one without a system because I was heavy and slow. Well, my Master told me the same thing, but I saw how the others talked when I came home. They seem like they became accomplished warriors."

"Not all of them," I said. "Some have not returned and others are quiet like us."

"Han Erh is always quiet," Denju reminded me. "But I wouldn't be surprised if he learned a whole system. Most bets are set on him winning tomorrow."

"I've no doubt," I said. "Let's go and find some of the other ones who aren't showing off. Maybe they feel like we do and we can encourage each other." Actually I just felt better knowing I was not the only one who was afraid.

"What if we're the only ones?" Denju asked. Then he shrugged and smiled as we began to search for others. We found six others like ourselves. Cheng Ner, who netted fish in Wulin Lake with his father and brothers, was the first we talked to. He had studied the broadsword and Pushing Hand system in Jangtoh.

He laughed when first I came up to him, "I heard that you tried to fight everyone in Jangtoh, Chu Jeng. You became a sort of legend in the city!" Cheng Ner and Denju laughed hard at me and I felt my cheeks redden.

"Well, I found a great teacher," I said in my defense. "Master Kanoh, teacher of Draka Von." Both of them stopped laughing immediately.

After a moment of silence, Cheng Ner said, "That's a bit hard to believe, Jeng, but I have never known you to lie. You really studied with Draka Von's teacher?"

Denju said, "It is said Draka Von's teacher lives in a deep cavern with his Master, a celestial dragon more than ten-thousand years old."

I just shook my head and we walked on in search of others while Denju told Cheng Ner our plan. We next ran into Kor Den, the tall, lanky son of a farmer. We found him manning a pie table with his pretty younger sister, Shenya. He guzzled down the last third of an oversized mug of ale as we approached the table.

"Kor Den, what are you doing drinking like that?" I said. "You should keep your strength intact for tomorrow."

Denju smiled and asked Kor Den's sister, "May we borrow your warrior brother for a while?" The young lady blushed and nodded, smiling back at him. Kor Den stepped out from behind the table with a slightly suspicious look. He walked away with us and Denju asked him, "Are you nervous about tomorrow?"

Kor Den answered, "I suppose I am. Aren't you?"

"We all are," Cheng Ner answered

"Even you?" Den asked Denju.

"I was quite scared until I started talking to Chu Jeng and Cheng Ner," he answered with relief showing in his voice. "Tell me, Kor Den. Did you learn a whole fighting system?"

"No," the lanky young man answered slowly. The ale began to show itself in his speech. "I studied the crane system with Master Sil Garn of the

41

Mountain Crane School in Paigen City. I also studied spear and steel chain, but I didn't even have time to delve below the surface of the style. A year isn't enough!" Then he whispered, "The Elders were wrong." He looked around and added, "Maybe we all should…"

Denju shook his head and the lanky man fell silent.

We walked on talking and gathering our quiet compatriots. We came across Torin Feng of the Praying Mantis system, just as he finished winning a goat milking contest. Ben Jin followed us distantly and warily for some time, watching from the shadows until curiosity overcame him and he asked us what we were up to. Ben Jin was barely taller than I and only a little stockier, but quite strong despite his small size.

"Have you performed any demonstrations today?" I asked him.

"Only a fool exposes his powers before a fight," he answered with a proverb.

"He sounds like my Master!" Den, Denju and Feng all blurted at once. We all laughed together and Denju Rehn explained the situation we all shared to Ben Jin. He laughed uncontrollably then suddenly ran up Denju's body as if it were a tree. Squatting on the bear-like man's shoulders, Jin pretended to pick and eat fleas from his hair.

Torin Feng laughed at the little man's antics and said, "Let me risk a wild guess. Ah, you studied a monkey system of fighting."

"I studied Monkey Fist and staff with Koren Jang of the Five Star Monkey School in Chulin, way to the south," Ben Jin declared proudly, still pretending to pick fleas from Denju's hair.

"Looks like you ate well, too," Torin Feng mocked. "I recognize the famous monkey school foraging technique."

Jin instantly leapt from Denju's shoulders, giggling and cursing as he chased Torin Feng across the market circle. We all ran after them, laughing and shouting encouragement to one or the other. It was then that I noticed that these young men were very different from the young men who had left Sanjurra village one year before. I could see it in the sudden, lightning-fast movements of Torin Feng as he ran and dodged his fluid, deceptive monkey-style pursuer. I wondered what trials and training regimens they had gone through in their studies. Ben Jin was as proud of his Master and his style as we all were of ours, even though none of us had finished a whole system. At last Torin Feng came to an instant stop. Ben Jin tumbled past him and lashed out with a playful kick toward the mantis artist's ribs. Feng instantly swept the kick away with a mantis hand block. The crowd in the market circle broke into applause and enthusiastic cheers.

"That's the best demonstration I have seen all day!" Elder Gazen shouted, clapping his gnarled old hands. The crowd cheered its agreement and gathered closer. It was all Feng and Jin could do to slip away from the mob. We found them later, crouched behind the ale wagon, discussing fighting strategies.

"Kanu Rahn is with us," I told the pair, interrupting their discussion. "He studied the eagle system with a famous old Master in the Iron Hills of Hujay Province. Perhaps you have heard of Master Tienjin Kahn?"

Ben Jin stood up and said, "I heard my Master say that Tienjin Kahn was reported to have died in battle, years ago."

Kanu Rahn shook his head and leapt up into the air. His leg flashed out in a circling kick that seemed to keep him afloat for an unnatural long time. He came down like a diving eagle and thrust his talon-like fingers deep into the thick sod. Standing up with a large piece of sod in each hand, he closed his curved fingers, squeezing the sod through them like soft clay. He smiled and said, "Master is alive and well in the Iron Hills."

"Did you finish your system?" Ben Jin asked with wide eyes.

"Not even close," Kanu Rahn answered. "Master Tienjin could crush rocks with his talon hand strikes. What I do falls pitifully short of his least efforts. I saw my neighbor, Gar Jeng when I first came home last night. He says he didn't finish his system either. He studied a throwing, choking and grappling system called Coiling Serpent."

"Where is he now?" Denju asked.

"I don't know," Kanu Rahn replied. "He said he would come to the festival, but 'nobody sees a snake that wants to hide'."

We kept our eyes open for Gar Jeng. Eventually we found him in hiding, much to his immediate disappointment. But his mood brightened up when he shared in our little conspiracy to bolster each others' confidence. We eventually ran into Han Erh. He was not alone, though he looked like he wanted to be, so we did not push our way through the throng of family members and girls to try to talk to him. They kept pleading with him to demonstrate more of his art. We left him to their "Oohs!" and "Ahhs!" The eight of us; Denju, Ner, Den, Feng, Jin, Rahn, Jeng and I, stuck together like brothers until the festival began to slow down. It appeared that the other men of the quest were too mobbed with admirers to get together much. We talked of our trials and training. We all had stories to tell, some of them very funny and mostly at our own expenses. The thing that drew us together most was not the remarkable similarities of our experiences. It was that we had all changed so much that we did not quite fit in with the villagers any longer.

43

Late that night, when we parted, Denju said, "I wish each one of you the best of luck and all the protection of Heaven. I will do my best to defeat each one of you as we promised the Elders one year ago. I just don't want to hurt anybody." We repeated our own versions of Denju's sentiment and reluctantly parted ways in silence.

When I reached my home, Mother and Father were in bed. I called for them quietly, but they were already asleep. Exhaustion hit me suddenly. It hit me both emotionally and physically. And fear struck me along with the weariness. I remembered that I never fought with my Master even once, while each of the others said he had fought with his fellow students and with his Master many times. Several of them said they had even fought and defeated robbers on the way home. I was the only one with no successful fighting experience at all. I picked up a sheet of paper and a pen to write a note to my parents. I would tell them I had to leave in the night to prevent my poor performance in the tournament from shaming them. I must have stared at that blank paper for an hour. At last I remembered staring at blank sheets of paper in another time and place. My reverence for Master Kanoh and his stern will gave me the resolve to outweigh my fears. I put the paper away and collapsed into bed. I would fight my one fight tomorrow and be taken quietly out of the tournament. I supposed it would not be so bad as long as I was just one inconspicuous loser in a crowd of nineteen losers.

7 - TOURNAMENT

The first day of spring had come, and with it came a deepening of my gut-wrenching dread. Every man, woman and child of Sanjurra village and the surrounding houses had gathered in the market circle for the tournament. They waited murmuring and shuffling for the first rays of the rising sun to touch a red banner at the top of a fifty-foot pole. The banner bore a single word; *Champion*. It was a reminder that there were to be no honors for second place that day. For reasons unknown, only seventeen of the original men of the quest returned to Sanjurra for the tournament. I sat next to Denju Rehn along with the rest of the contestants on a low bench that was constructed for the tournament and set there during the night. A smooth ring of heavy curved timbers was firmly anchored to the center of the market circle just ten feet north of us. The timbers were about eight inches by eight inches and each about ten feet long as they lay end to end on the ground to form the circle. The ring was set there during the night with heavy iron spikes driven through the timbers into the ground. Elder Korenda sat with the other Elders on a raised wooden platform to the north of the fighting ring.

The banner began to glow bright red at its uppermost tip and Elder Korenda stood up. He raised his arms to silence the crowd. Everybody became still. The silence was interrupted only by a man coughing lightly into his sleeve.

Elder Korenda bowed before the crowd and then spoke in his loudest, most official voice, "Greetings to all who long for the peace and prosperity of old. This beautiful morning speaks to us with the promise of spring. Our fields are sprouting with fresh growth. Our livestock are tending their many young or are heavy with pending birth. In the past this promise of spring drew bandits and others to steal and eat out of the fruit of our labor. This day, the promise of spring is different for us. This day brings to us a promise of bounty not known since my grandfather's time in this very village. The dawning of this day brings us a promise like none we have ever known because seventeen warriors sit here in our midst. Warriors who will fight this day for the title of Champion of Sanjurra; village protector. The champion will teach his war art to the others, and they in turn to all our able youth. The day will come soon when our village and the surrounding region will be free of banditry; free of fear; free to prosper in peace!"

The crowd began to cheer. The contestants sat in silence as the village priest sprinkled the fighting ring with sacred water and said his blessing. I wondered how embarrassingly I would be defeated in front of all the people.

Denju leaned toward me and spoke below the din of the crowd, "I think everybody is going to fight very hard. I don't want to give up my Master's style if I lose!" His words scared me so bad I felt like throwing up. He looked at my face and said, "Relax, Jeng. You're among those who care for you. I swear. It felt last night like we were all brothers. Do you understand what I'm saying?"

I nodded and smiled, but felt like running away. There was nothing for huge, well-muscled, Denju to fear from his little brothers of the quest.

Elder Korenda silenced the crowd once again and continued, "Our village doctor is present in the event that one of the competitors is injured. The Council of Elders has painted the names, fighting styles, masters and places of study of each of the seventeen fighters on individual wooden tiles. They placed the tiles into this black bag." He motioned to Elder Kwan who stood smiling and raised the bag for all to see. "Heaven will decide by lot who the first two fighters will be." On his signal, Elder Kwan slowly and ceremoniously brought the bag to him. Without looking, Elder Korenda pulled back his sleeve and reached into the bag. He slowly churned the tiles, over and over then stopped with a suddenness that caused my stomach to jump. I hoped I would be chosen first, along with Han Erh. That way my suffering would be over right away and I would be less shamed by losing to the best of the village. Elder Korenda drew the tile from the bag and said, "The first fighter will be Gis Erh, who studied the Leopard system and the saber under Gendra Ner in the imperial Capitol, Paigen City."

Gis Erh stood up slowly and walked to the center of the ring. He wore an orange banner over his shoulder with three leopard's rosettes in a triangular pattern on the front and back. Turning to the Elders, he set his right knee to the ground and bowed his head as a symbol of his service to the village and its people. The people cheered for him. His family and friends shouted his name as he stood and backed to the edge of the ring.

Elder Korenda reached back into the bag. Again the slow dramatic churning of tiles and abrupt stop before he drew the next tile. I could hardly breathe. "The next fighter will be... Rume Lak, who studied the Iron Monkey system and the cane under Master Han Li in Gansau City."

The crowd cheered again as Rume Lak walked into the circle and showed his fealty as his competitor had done. He wore farmer's clothes and nobody would guess by looking at him that he was trained to do anything but farming. His name was shouted with hope and wishes for luck.

Elder Korenda raised his arms to hush the anxious crowd and spoke again, "Both of these fighters showed us some of their impressive war arts yesterday in the market circle. Now only one of them will earn the right to continue in the contest." The fighters turned to face each other and Elder Korenda clapped his hands once. The crowd hushed immediately and all attention was locked on the men in the fighting ring.

Gis Erh assumed a fighting cat stance and brought his hands up to guard with flattened tiger claws. He began to inch carefully toward Rume Lak.

"What a sloppy, weak cat stance!" I whispered to Denju. I figured he would agree with me since he had studied a tiger and crane system and would know what a good cat stance was.

Instead, he said, "I don't see anything wrong with it." Then he added, "Notice how the fingers of his claws are flattened. I have heard that the leopard flattens most of its hand forms. Master told me that the leopard system is three times faster than the tiger, but not as strong."

Only when Gis Erh reached the center of the ring did Rume Lak react. The monkey warrior assumed a very low and slightly twisted fighting horse stance. He squared his shoulders toward his opponent and dropped more of his weight to his rear leg. It was very different from the more sideways horse I was taught with the weight distributed evenly on both feet. His guard was also very different from mine and he continually shuffled forward and back while weaving and bobbing. Sometimes he touched one or both of his fists to the ground. Were I to have done any of the things he was doing, Master Kanoh would have beat me while shouting a barrage of invective to melt stone like ice.

The two warriors closed distance cautiously with Rume Lak, the monkey man, trying to circle and deceive Gis Erh, the leopard man. Rume Lak feigned a movement to his left and, just when Gis Erh began to adjust his stance to the movement, rolled through the leopard man's legs. Gis Erh jumped over the monkey, trying to roll forward to escape the attack, but the monkey caught one of the leopard's leggings in his hand. For a moment, I thought Gis Erh's neck would break as his roll stopped at precisely the wrong time. But he quickly slid his right shoulder underneath him and twisted out of the trap. Using his powerful left hamstring, he delivered a sharp heel hook to the monkey's arm. Then he pushed himself up from the ground, assumed his cat stance and attacked the rising monkey with a series of fast kicks. The monkey blocked the kicks while backing quickly away from the rushing leopard. When the monkey reached the edge of the ring, I thought he would step out and lose the match. Instead he took a snapping kick to the groin in order to grab the leopard's right sleeve. His deception was perfect and I immediately saw the danger to the leopard. I had listened to too many stories from Master Kanoh not to recognize it. I had been thrown similarly and painfully in his demonstrations of basic throws. The monkey instantly slipped beneath the leopard's barrage and pulled down on his sleeve while thrusting a kick up into his groin. The leopard rose into the air, but somehow twisted to land on his feet. He had one foot in the ring and the other on the wooden circle. The monkey tried to kick him out of the ring but the leopard ran a few steps down the curved wooden beam. He balanced for a moment and then both his hands went to his groin as he bent over and started to collapse. The monkey quickly ran to push the seemingly helpless leopard out of the ring. When he came within striking range, the leopard spun on the beam, swept the monkey's hands down and leopard punched him in the side of the neck. The monkey's eyes rolled back and he collapsed to the dirt.

Rume Lak came back to consciousness and sat up groggily before doctor Gen Li reached his side. Gis Erh stepped off the wooden fighting ring, turned to the Elders and gave the sign of his fealty to the village again.

"I bet that hurt," Denju said with a slight nervous quiver in his voice.

"I've taken worse," I said, as Elder Korenda declared Gis Erh the winner of the first bout. The crowd cheered the winner.

Rume Lak stood up shakily and the crowd began to cheer again. I heard the groaning of wheels and turned to see the crowd parting behind me for the ale wagon. A different kind of cheer rose up as the first keg was tapped. The whole event was so different and new and festive that it seemed the simple people of the village did not quite know what to do but cheer and have a good time. The ring was raked clean of the last fight, then the priest blessed and sprinkled it for the next.

The crowd hushed as Elder Korenda reached into the black bag for the name of the next fighter. I silently prayed it would be I to fight next; so that I could get it over with soon.

Korenda hushed the crowd and called out loudly and with all ceremony, "The next fighter will be Kor Den who studied the Mountain Crane system, the spear and the steel chain under Master Sil Garn in Paigen City." Drawing the next tile, he said, "Kor Den's opponent will be Amon Deng who studied the Black Tiger system under Master Tienja Von in Gwongen City, the capitol of our own Gurin Province." After their signs of fealty, the fighters stood facing each other from opposite sides of the ring. Korenda clapped his hands once.

"This should be interesting," Denju said quietly. "The tiger will try to get close and use his aggressive power. The Crane's way is to avoid direct confrontation and dodge to the side or slip away while striking his opponent from a distance. I studied a mixed tiger and crane system. I've never watched fighters from the two opposing animal systems go against each other."

Denju was right. The tiger aggressively pursued the crane while the crane seemed to ride the air and avoid the tiger's punches, kicks and sweeping claws. The tiger's strikes, though not landing on target, seemed to be much more powerful than the crane's. Then lanky Kor Den used his superior reach to swing gracefully over one of Amon Deng's hard sweeping back fist blows. Kor Den used the non-damaging crane feathers technique to lightly rake his fingers across the tiger's eyes. The tiger was temporarily blinded and the tall skinny crane took full advantage of the situation. Dropping his hands to the ground, he swept his leg in a hard fast arc through the tiger's legs. Amon Deng's feet flew up as high as his chest before his body started down. The whole bench of competitors instantly stood up just as Amon Deng's upper back and shoulders crashed into the ground. A low murmur of sympathy swept through the crowd.

There was a moment of silence as Doctor Gen Li stepped into the ring and made his way toward the fallen tiger. Then he scrambled back out as the tiger leapt to his feet and raised his guard. The crowd sighed its relief, and the crane attacked before the tiger regained his breath. Kor Den landed a few hard whirling crane fist blows to the tiger's head, but could not effectively strike his body. The tiger was regaining his breath even though a couple of the head shots he took were dizzying. Suddenly he grasped the tiring crane's left forearm with his right hand and squeezed. Kor Den groaned with pain and lashed out with a front snap kick. Amon Deng dug into a nearly flat horse stance and pulled the crane's arm to the side, throwing his kick off target. The Tiger grimaced and growled as he squeezed harder and harder, showing his teeth like an animal as he forced the crane toward the ground.

Kor Den fell to his knees and struggled with the crushing pain for some time before shouting, "I yield! I yield!"

Amon Deng switched his grip to the crane man's hand and helped him to his feet. Kor Den hugged the mighty tiger man and they said a few words to each other that none could hear above the din of the cheering crowd.

Elder Korenda declared, "Amon Deng of the Black Tiger system has won the second bout of this championship!"

Amon Deng led Kor Den out of the ring to Doctor Gen. Even from where we sat, Denju and I could see a terrible bruise already forming on Kor Den's forearm as the doctor pulled back his sleeve.

"Heaven's gain!" Denju blurted out. "What a grip! I hope someone takes him out before I have to fight him!"

His statement did wonders for my mood. I wanted to tell him to shut up. I wanted to tell him that any person who took the tiger out would be no safer to fight than the tiger he had already beaten. Denju had a heart as big as a mountain, but he sometimes did not think things out very thoroughly. I decided that I would yield long before I would ever let somebody make my arm look like Kor Den's.

A plump village-woman behind me said, "Oh, that's hideous! I wish all weapons and war arts could somehow be destroyed and forgotten, except those needed for the authorities to maintain safety and order."

My jaw dropped open in shock at the woman's ignorance. Half the fighters on the bench turned and glared at her or just looked in shock as I did.

Denju stood up and said to her, "Madam, your foolish belief in a fairytale world is more hideous than anything we will see here today."

"That's right!" Ben Jin added. "People like you enable the Tardor foreigners to enslave our people."

Gis Erh said to her, "Please back out of earshot if you are going to prattle on that way."

"What a fool!" another fighter muttered, almost too quietly for her to hear.

The woman covered her mouth with her hand and ran away, blushing.

The ring was raked and blessed for the third fight of the tournament and Korenda drew the tiles from his black bag. "The first fighter of this bout will be... Cheng Ner who studied the Pushing Hand system and the broadsword under Traku Jen in Jangtoh City. His worthy opponent will be Kanu Rahn who studied the Eagle system under the venerable Master Tienjin Kahn in the Iron Hills of Hujay Province."

The fighters gave their signs of fealty and backed to the edges of the ring. Elder Korenda clapped his signal and they assumed their stances, advancing slowly. Kanu Rahn moved toward his opponent with traditional crescent steps preserving the integrity of his horse. Cheng Ner, on the other hand, seemed to just walk fluidly toward the eagle man. When they met, Kanu Rahn dashed Cheng Ner's guard down and tried to punch him in the head. Cheng Ner offered no resistance to the eagle's movement. Instead, he let his arms circle to dash the eagle's arms down in turn. Then he circled his own hands in, down and then up under the eagle's rising guard. Cheng Ner seemed to leave his hands on the eagle's ribs for a moment then he thrust his whole body upward. Kanu Rahn grunted loudly as his feet lifted off the ground. He flew from the center of the ring to the edge, barely missing the wooden beams with his head as his back slapped into the dirt.

Four times Kanu Rahn rushed Cheng Ner with his refined eagle attacks. Four times he flew backwards through the air and crashed to the ground. A man who did not know how to break his fall would have been hurt and probably defeated by any of those falls. The eagle's next attack dashed Cheng Ner's head back, but left his arms trapped in Ner's grip. With a sudden twist, Cheng Ner threw the eagle spiraling sideways into the dirt. Kanu Rahn clambered slowly to his feet. His pain was obvious to all. Then Cheng Ner attacked with blood trickling down his face from the eagle's only hit. Cheng Ner absorbed a warding blow from the eagle and spun him around for an arm bar. The situation looked hopeless for the eagle. Then he stomped on Cheng Ner's foot and launched himself through the air and away from his opponent. At first I thought Cheng Ner had pushed the eagle again, but when Kanu Rahn spun around he yanked Cheng Ner forward into a stunning palm heel strike to the head. Cheng Ner looked dazed beyond hope, but the eagle finished his counterattack by chopping the back of Cheng Ner's neck with the side of his hand and then kicking him in the ribs. Cheng Ner crumpled into a ball on the ground and did not move.

Doctor Li rushed to the fallen warrior as Elder Korenda declared Kanu Rahn the winner. It took nearly a quarter hour before Cheng Ner could stand and walk away. The crowd cheered at his recovery. The ale flowed freely and a wagering table was set up to facilitate the already frenzied betting.

Before the contest, I had thought that Master Kanoh had taught me every possible way to hit, block and kick. Watching the fighters in the contest showed me that my Iron Fist style lacked a few basics, though not many. The thought that they could do things that I could not, made me a little envious. I became intensely interested to see more of what the other styles contained.

Again the villagers prepared the ring and Korenda raised his official voice. "The next fighter will be Ben Jin who studied the Five Star Monkey Fist system and the long staff under Master Koren Jang in Chulin City. His opponent will be Tenju Gen who studied the White Dragon system, the Fire Wind and the Water Palm under… a Master he refused to name and in a place he refused to reveal." The crowd went totally silent as Tenju Gen walked to the center of the ring to deeply and respectfully bend his knee and neck in fealty.

"Why the secrecy with your Elders?" Korenda asked the man.

Tenju Gen stood and answered, "It is the way of my Master, Sir. I must respect his ways of transformation, secrecy and honor."

Korenda gave one slow grim nod, and the dragon man walked to the edge of the ring opposite Ben Jin. I guessed by the look on Elder Korenda's face that he was not pleased that any villager should respect the ways of an outsider above those of the village and its Elders. He clapped his hands as if very angry and the bout began.

Ben Jin assumed the strange fighting horse stance of the monkey system and began to deceptively weave and bob his way toward the dragon. I marveled that a monkey stylist from Chulin City, nearly three hundred miles south of Sanjurra, should move so much like another kind of monkey stylist from Gansau, which is even a farther distance to the north. Though the monkey was deceptive in his movements, the dragon was deceptive in his stillness; almost hard to look at steadily. When the monkey drew close, he lashed out at the dragon with an upward thrusting kick from his low stance. The look on the monkey's face showed me that he thought his kick should have connected. The dragon simply twisted away from the blow, moving neither too much nor too little. Several more blows were avoided in the same way. Then the monkey rushed the dragon with a sort of push. The dragon disappeared below the monkey's assault, grabbing his wrists and thrusting a foot into his belly. The action in the ring seemed to go into slow motion as I watched a helpless, horrified look form on the monkey's face. The dragon seemed to be made of a mist that could not be touched, but he could certainly touch. The monkey's feet swung up behind him and high over his head as he released a low and ominous scream. He could have easily rolled out of the fall except that the dragon would not let go of his wrists. The monkey's entire back and legs slapped into the ground making an ugly sound for how it must have hurt. The dragon let go of him and rolled away, neatly rising into a fine fighting horse with his guard up. Tenju Gen soon realized that there was no need for his guard as Ben Jin rolled groaning onto his belly and lay almost perfectly still.

Elder Korenda stood up and raised his arms and frowned, saying, "Tenju Gen is the victor in this bout."

Ben Jin raised himself slowly and began limping out of the ring before the doctor could reach his side. I looked at Denju who sat bug-eyed and gape-jawed. The wagering table went wild.

A fighter off to my left whispered, "He slapped him around like a spoiled child."

Korenda stared at the white Dragon for a moment and then called to the crowd, "We will take a short break and ring the town bell to reconvene the tournament."

The fighters all stood up and mostly dispersed as the people of Sanjurra broke into groups or crowded up to the wagering table.

I said to Denju, "There are so many ways to fight. I once thought that war art was just war art."

"It is," he said.

I corrected, "I mean that I thought war art was just one thing and that the only difference was that certain people were just better at it than others."

Denju frowned and said, "We discussed the differing styles last night."

"We talked mostly about philosophical differences. I didn't know the actual movements would be so different."

"Hmm. Yeah. That's right," Denju mumbled as he stretched his neck to see farther over the crowd.

"What are you looking at?" I asked.

"The same thing Korenda is looking at and he seems angry. He's watching Han Erh talk to Senya Dain and Tenju Gen. Elder Bakken is sneaking a listen behind the fighters like a cheap spy. What's it all about? They're like opposing forces preparing to go to war."

I asked him, "What do you suppose would be better; forcing your opponent to fight your kind of fight or knowing all styles so you can fight with any kind of strategy?"

"Huh?" Denju said, then turned from staring at the three dragon stylists and looked down at me. "Oh. I don't think you could learn all the styles in a lifetime. But, then I don't think you can always force your opponent to fight in the way you would like him to, either."

I thought for a moment and said, "I think there is some option between the two that would be best."

"Nonsense," he said. "You either fight the enemy at long range or short. That's all there is to it."

8 - ELIMINATION

We reassembled after the break and again my stomach churned as Elder Korenda reached into his black bag of terror. He pulled a tile and read it. "The first warrior of this fifth bout for Sanjurra Champion will be," he paused for dramatic effect, "Han Erh, who…" Several village girls screamed and Elder Korenda frowned at them. I just shook my head and wanted to crawl under the fighter's bench. Korenda continued, "Han Erh, who studied the Southern Dragon system under Master Viendu Ben in Sanghuei City, near the Husang Border Region." Elder Korenda was always proud to display his superior geography skills. He usually tried to talk as if he had traveled the world instead of studying maps, but we all knew better, even if respect kept us from saying so. "Han Erh's worthy opponent will be Kavel Tom who studied the Mountain Long Fist under Master Jao Mun in the Ganju Mountains to the north and west of our region."

"Poor Tom," I said to Denju. "Look at his face. Well, he should be glad to lose to Han Erh rather than anyone else. Perhaps some pretty girl will want to hug him just because Han Erh's fists bounced him around."

Denju let out a low chuckle, then looked over at Tenju Gen sitting placidly on the bench and went silent. I thought then that perhaps he felt some of the fear that I felt. I quit trying to humor him and concentrated on my own predicament. It suddenly did not seem as bad though, knowing that at least two of the others felt as miserable as I did.

Elder Korenda clapped his hands and Han Erh walked toward his opponent and formed a horse stance. Kavel Tom assumed a fighting stance and advanced on Han Erh. As they neared the center of the ring, Kavel Tom rushed Han Erh, throwing a fast series of long punches and kicks. The strikes were an intricate mix of straight and curved blows. It looked like a good attack, but Han Erh retreated just out of range and watched while his opponent attacked. Then Han Erh cut right through the attack with a straight punch of his forward hand; twisting his shoulders for greater reach and power. The blow landed on Kavel Tom's sternum and sent him dazed and gasping to the ground. He probably would have gotten back up and continued after a few moments to recover if Han Erh would have let him. Instead, Han Erh did the merciful thing by descending on Kavel Tom, pinning him to the ground with his guard immobilized and threatening another punch.

"I Yield!" Kavel Tom shouted.

Han Erh helped Kavel Tom to his feet and they briefly embraced as Korenda said, "Han Erh of the Southern Dragon system is the winner!" The crowd shouted and cheered. When Han Erh reached the edge of the ring, a crowd of mostly female admirers thronged him, much to his obvious displeasure. I noticed that Han Rinya was not among them.

I had been nervous and sick for so long that I was becoming numb. I no longer prayed it would be my tile when Elder Korenda reached into that black bag. I knew the number of tiles in the bag had been reduced by ten already. My chances were two in seven that I would be chosen on the next drawing. The crowd had emptied six kegs and more than a few men had grown somewhat unruly with all the ale and unusual excitement. The Elders told the crowd to back up from the ring, which they did obediently. However, they felt they could stand, murmuring, jostling and jabbering, right behind the competitor's bench. A heated discussion was taking place directly behind me about the possibility of a death occurring in the tournament. One of the sodden debaters gestured in his anger, forgetting that his hand held a full mug of ale. I jumped forward off the bench only after receiving an ample wash of cool frothy ale down my back. As if on cue, the whole bench of fighters stood up and began sternly warning the crowd to back up. They complied immediately. I guess I was not the only one of the fighters irritated with the crowd, even if I was the only one who smelled like a used keg.

I sat down and said to Denju, "What is wrong with those slobs? You would think they had never seen a fight before!" Then I remembered that the villagers were simple, peaceful people who were likely to see perhaps only a handful of clumsy, untrained fights in an entire lifetime. The spectacle before them was both stunning and magical in their eyes. Perhaps it even seemed threatening to some of them.

Elder Korenda drew a tile from the bag. I hardly paid attention as I struggled to wring ale from the back of my tunic. He made his announcement loudly. "The first fighter of this sixth bout will be Denju Rehn who studied the Tiger and Crane system under Master Kahl Sem in Gwongen City."

I watched my friend rise slowly from his seat with darkening eyes. He walked to the ring and stepped into it. Denju was nearly the tallest of those chosen for the quest and was clearly the most muscular. I do not know why, but I feared for his safety then. I suppose it may have been that he was so kindhearted and innocent of mind. I wondered who of the remaining contestants would be chosen to go against him, then felt the blood drain from my head as I realized I might be the one chosen.

Korenda pulled a tile from the bag. I wished I could run up there and stop him from reading it. "Denju Rehn's worthy opponent will be Torin Feng who studied the Praying Mantis system under the venerable old Master Chien Dru in Bintu Village on the eastern shore of Shirelin Lake."

Several inebriated people laughed as Korenda named the diminutive Torin Feng as Denju's opponent. They did not understand that in a real fight Torin Feng would do quite nicely against the burly Denju. I had learned the night before that the praying mantis system is designed for women and small men to use against larger, stronger opponents. Unfortunately for Torin Feng, it was not a real fight against a big, strong attacker. It was a non-lethal match against a big, strong friend. Thus, most of Torin Feng's strikes were too deadly or crippling to use in the tournament. The dilemma Feng knew he was in showed in his face.

Korenda glared at those who had laughed and then clapped his hands once. Sometime after the fight commenced, I could see that Denju Rehn was taking it easy on Torin Feng, but then the smaller man struck Denju lightning-fast in the solar plexus with a sharp middle knuckle punch. It took the wind from Denju's lungs. I had never seen anyone's arms move as fast as Torin Feng's. Even Master Kanoh did not move as fast as Torin Feng, but speed was not the specialty of the Iron Fist system. I remembered Torin Feng telling me the night before that speed is the primary quality of the mantis, followed by patience, timing, perception and precision.

The mantis waited, eerily still, with his arms drawn close to his chest and his hands bent sharply down at the wrists. He cocked his head to the side as he stood in a long bow stance and watched his enormous opponent circle him warily. I could see elements in Denju's movements of both the tiger and the crane stylists I had seen earlier. When Denju attacked, the mantis never tried to dash his own arms against his opponents. Instead he used the bigger man's arms as levers to maneuver himself around quickly. He struck with blinding speed under Denju's ribs with pointed attacks. I saw Denju wince in pain several times, but since the mantis was disallowed his best weapons, I knew Denju would not be felled. Then Denju landed a palm heel blow to the mantis man's shoulder, which lifted his feet off the ground and threw him into a staggering run. When the mantis recovered, he held his guard differently, obviously in pain. Denju closed on him and leapt forward with animal-like aggression. The mantis caught a terrible punch to the forehead and staggered backward, arms flailing desperately for balance. He turned round as his arms fell to his sides and his knees buckled, dropping his limp form to the ground.

Elder Korenda declared the winner as Denju ran to his friend and lifted him like a child in his arms. He carried him halfway to Doctor Li who ran from the edge of the ring. Blood poured freely from Torin Feng's forehead, cascading over Denju's arm and running down his leggings.

"I'm sorry, Feng," Denju said. Then looking at Doctor Li, he said, "I should have just pushed him out of the ring."

Without stopping his rapidly working hands, the doctor tried to reassure Denju Rehn with, "You were just as cautious as he was, son. There is no need to blame yourself." Several men helped the doctor to carry Torin Feng into merchant Gener's general store. Denju came and sat down beside me. His hands were shaking and he did not say a thing. I wanted to say something to comfort him, but I could not find the words. It didn't seem like he wanted to talk anyway, so I just kept quiet. I knew my time in the ring had to be coming soon. The odds had moved up to two in five.

When the time came, Elder Korenda reached into the bag and announced the next fighter, "The first fighter of this seventh bout of our village tournament will be Chu Jeng who studied the Iron Fist system under Master Kanoh Feng on Lungshan Mountain." He frowned, obviously not knowing where Lungshan Mountain was. Nobody knew where the remote mountain was, but Master Kanoh, Draka Von and I. Thinking about the secrecy of the mountain retreat, I desperately longed to be there with my Master. I remembered the outlandish trials and tests he had put me through; things I would never have thought humanly possible to accomplish. But I did accomplish them in the secret place that stumped Korenda's proud geographic mastery. Suddenly it hit me that the contests in the fighting ring were not half as difficult as most of the things Master Kanoh had put me through, though the ring was obviously more dangerous.

Elder Korenda drew another tile and continued, "His worthy opponent will be Onde Tor who studied the Whirling Fists system and the double broadsword under Master Draku Yen in Gwongen City." After Onde Tor and I made our signs of fealty and backed to opposing sides of the ring, Korenda clapped his hands.

Onde Tor took four quick steps to the center of the ring and assumed a sloppy-looking fighting horse stance. I took two steps forward and assumed a deep horse. I noticed my forward guard shaking, almost imperceptibly, and I tried to focus my full attention on Onde Tor. I saw his eyes light up just before he attacked. Master Kanoh always said that the best fighters see another fighter's eyes light up just before they attack. In that way they can attack first and stifle their enemy's movements while their spirit is still focused on the pending attack. "The timing is critical" he had told me. He ended it with his usual admonition that I remember it. I did remember, and launched myself forward into a leaping side thrust kick at just the precise moment. Onde Tor blocked the kick with both arms, but it plowed through his blocks and threw him backward into the air with a pained grunt. He came down on his feet, stumbling helplessly backward and tripped over the wooden edge of the ring. He fell flat on his back in the fastest defeat of the tournament thus far. Nobody cheered my victory. The silence made me fear that I had done something terribly wrong.

When I turned toward the fighters' bench, I saw that they were all on their feet gaping at me. The crowd gaped along with them, then started to cheer much louder than they had after any of the other fights. Onde Tor stood up and slowly, clumsily brushed the dirt off his clothes. He seemed to be having some difficulty breathing as he slowly walked back toward the fighters' bench. I noticed Torin Feng standing and weakly cheering along with the rest of the fighters. His head was bandaged and his face was very pale. Turning to genuflect to my Elders again, I saw my father's brothers carrying him in triumph on their shoulders. A throng of my mother, cousins and aunts followed them, raising their fists and cheering. I walked back to my seat in a daze. It was my thirty-fourth fight and my first win.

When I reached the bench, Denju slapped me on the back, almost knocking me down and joked, "Great Kick, Jeng! I hope I don't have to fight you next."

I smiled and sat down trying to figure out what had happened in the fight. Why had it been so easy?

The next fight came quickly, since there was not much raking to do in the ring. Elder Korenda drew two tiles and introduced the fighters. "The first fighter of this eighth bout will be Gar Jeng who studied the Coiling Serpent system under Master Denmin Rahn in Banzu City. He will face Trou Gom who studied the Cobra system and the double broadsword under Master Hong Jem in Gwenje City "

I became intensely interested in how two warriors of the snake system would fight each other. I wondered if the Coiling Serpent system would differ greatly from the Cobra system or if they would somehow cancel each other out. Gar Jeng assumed a strange twisted stance and seemed almost to slither across the fighting ring toward Trou Gom, the cobra man. Trou Gom slid his right foot forward to a very deep bow stance and brought his hands to an open guard. He breathed out loudly, almost like the hiss of a snake. The eerie hissing sound was matched by his glassy, cold-looking eyes. He seemed transformed into something I could barely recognize as the familiar Trou Gom of my home village.

Gar Jeng slithered his way to close range with his opponent and then stopped. Both fighters held their very different stances and eyed each other, swaying gently, almost imperceptibly. It seemed an unnaturally long wait, as if the fighters had secretly planned to play a trick on the crowd. Then Gar Jeng lunged forward deceptively fast. I did not see the movement until he was almost on top of Trou Gom. Gar Jeng tried to take hold of Trou Gom's arm and hook his own leg around his opponent's. Trou Gom twisted his arm and body out of Jeng's way and swung his foot around like a serpent's tail. Trou Gom's heel thudded into Jeng's back, making a sound like a drum. Not seeming to feel the blow, Gar Jeng reached between Trou Gom's legs from the rear and grabbed his belt. Jeng's other arm instantly encircled Trou Gom's neck and tightened as he lifted his opponent off the ground. I winced for Trou Gom, knowing the pressure on his groin and throat must have been terrible.

Trou Gom's eyes bulged and his mouth opened in a silent scream as the arm around his neck constricted more tightly. Then Trou Gom simultaneously delivered a crushing right elbow to the coiling serpent's ribs and reached back over his own right shoulder to left finger-jab his attacker's neck. Gar Jeng made the mistake of twisting his head left and away from the neck jab. Trou Gom reversed his movement, left elbowed Jeng's ribs and reached over his left shoulder with his right hand to grab Jeng's cheek. Trou Gom's thumb stretched his opponent's cheek so far out from the inside that I thought it would soon tear its way through his flesh.

Gar Jeng was clearly hurt by Trou Gom's counter attack. He let go of Trou Gom's belt and reached his arm up under Trou Gom's armpit and around his neck as he tore his face loose of his hand. He then used the leverage of his arm against Trou Gom's neck to throw him downward into a rising knee strike into his back. Trou Gom gave with the knee strike and fell to the ground. Gar Jeng instantly fell toward Trou Gom for a grappling maneuver, but the cobra lashed out with his foot and connected hard on the side of Jeng's face. The kick spun him entirely off course and Trou Gom was on his feet, gasping for breath. He charged the recovering Gar Jeng with multiple knifehand chops, whirling in and out of their own circles in serpentine patterns. Gar Jeng backed up and desperately blocked most of the blows with his own heavy blocks. The sound of their bodies and arms slapping against each other was like a frenzied song beaten out on a corpse. The blows were hurting Jeng and weakening him. Trou Gom almost chased Gar Jeng out of the ring, but he made the mistake of looking down to check his progress toward the wooden edge of the ring. Gar Jeng instantly grabbed hold of one of Trou Gom's wrists and violently jerked himself around to his back. He threw Trou Gom to the ground and fell on him in a writhing tangle before he could react. It took only seconds before Gar Jeng had Trou Gom in a deadly, crushing and choking hold.

Trou Gom's face quickly turned a frightening red and his eyes bulged out like eggs. I realized just before the Elders screamed for Gar Jeng to stop, that Trou Gom had no way of escaping or calling out that he wanted to yield. Doctor Li was running toward the ring when Gar Jeng seemed to sense the warnings around him and let go of his opponent. Trou Gom choked and sputtered for a few moments, but was otherwise uninjured.

Elder Korenda was visibly unnerved by the strange inhuman fight of the snake warriors. He stood and his voice shook as he said, "Gar Jeng is the winner of this contest."

Gar Jeng and Trou Gom embraced each other and walked back to the fighters' bench, talking about their love of snakes and ignoring everybody else as if they were the only two living creatures for miles around.

There was only one fighter left in Elder Korenda's black bag; Senya Dain. Tall and quiet, Senya Dain was the oldest of the men of the quest. He was thirty years old, hardly a youth like the rest of us, but he insisted on competing for the quest, five seasons ago when the whole idea started. Dain had lost his wife and children to a fire started by Warlord Kang's disgruntled *tax collectors* only two years before the winter of the competition. He never took another wife or even talked much with his neighbors after the fire, though he was always as kind and polite as ever when one did have dealings with him. He rarely even left his rebuilt duck ranch, except to buy feed or sell ducks and eggs. The Elders could hardly refuse the lonely man's request. He made the list of twenty, went out into the world and returned with a dragon system, but remained nearly as quiet and withdrawn as before the quest.

It was long past noon when it came to the ninth fight of the tournament. Elder Korenda struggled to silence the hungry crowd. When he gained their attention, he said, "Our good neighbor, Senya Dain, is the last of the fighters left to fight. He studied the Green Dragon system, the throwing dart, the war sling and the throwing coin under Master Cheung Erh in Paigen City. The Elders are in agreement that Gis Erh will fight for a second time in these preliminary matches. He was chosen to fight against Senya Dain in this match because he has rested longer than any of the other winning fighters. The people are all hungry, I am sure." An affirmative shout and cheer rose up from the crowd. Korenda continued, smiling, "I ask you women to go home and prepare something to sustain our people and reward these brave fighters. We will rest from the tournament after this fight to partake of a small feast and then resume when we have supped." A wild cheer swept through the people and Korenda had a difficult time hushing them for the fight between Senya Dain and Gis Erh. On the Elder's signal, the warriors assumed their fighting stances and advanced in impressive watchfulness toward each other.

Senya Dain's horse stance was fairly good in its depth and alignment. He held his guard clean and steady as he shuffled with clearly showing confidence toward his opponent. He held an advantage over Gis Erh because he had already seen the leopard stylist fight against the iron monkey. Gis Erh seemed to want to test the green dragon's fighting style out before he launched a full attack. He feinted and ducked; lashed out from too great a distance then quickly retreated. All the while, he watched for some weakness or tendency in the dragon's method. Senya Dain shuffled steadily forward, revealing as little as possible of his fighting preferences. He seemed to be trying to edge Gis Erh closer to the beams of the ring.

Gis Erh glanced behind himself at the beams. They lay less than a full step away. He feigned to his right then darted left to avoid the trap. I had seen too many of his feints by then to believe his rightward movement. Apparently Senya Dain did not fall for the trick either. He stuck to the desperate leopard and launched a complex whirlwind of punches, claws, chops and kicks at him. Even Gis Erh's fast leopard style could not thwart the relentless multiple attacks. He recoiled while throwing his own daring counterattack at the dragon. He traveled a third of the way around the edge of ring, but the dragon would not let up. The dragon's harsh attacks swarmed their way through the leopard's formidable defense as it fell to fatigue and confusion. Gis Erh stepped out of the ring and nodded his acknowledgment that he was no match for Senya Dain.

Elder Korenda seemed much relieved that the last bout ended without injury or blood. He smiled and said, "Senya Dain of the Green Dragon system is the winner in this last bout of the first eliminations. The tiles of the following war artists will be put into the bag for the next four elimination matches; Amon Deng of the Black Tiger system, Chu Jeng of the Iron Fist system, Denju Rehn of the Tiger and Crane system, Gar Jeng of the Coiling Serpent system, Han Erh of the Southern Dragon system,

Kanu Rahn of the Eagle system, Senya Dain of the Green Dragon system and Tenju Gen of the White Dragon system. Congratulations, thus far, men."

The crowd cheered and shouted the names of competitors and the names of their systems. The cheering and reveling went on for perhaps half an hour before the Elders could regain control. By then, some of the women of the village were returning with food. The increasing appearance of food and tables helped to hush the rowdy crowd a bit.

Elder Korenda shielded his eyes from the high sun and shouted above the lingering shouts and talk, "The contests will commence two hours from now. Until then… let us feast!"

The crowd went wild. Many of those whose women had not yet returned with food hastened home to assist them. Several more kegs were rolled out from merchant, Gener's store, but only after a collection was taken up to pay him in advance.

9 - METTLE

Denju stood up from the bench, stretched his back and said, "I'm eating."

I followed him toward a table of baked goods and vegetables. "How can you eat, Denju? You may be fighting next."

"I'm hungry," he replied, as he grabbed a wooden bowl and began filling it with samples of everything within reach.

I said, "Look at the rest of the war artists who are still in the competition. None of them are making their way to the food tables."

"They are," he said, pointing out the fighters who had already been eliminated.

"Those men are not going to fight anymore," I said, then gave up as I watched him stuff a whole cornbread muffin in his mouth. I shook my head and changed the subject, saying, "Look Denju, some of those losing fighters seem defeated in spirit while others seem to be relieved that they are out of it."

Denju nodded without looking up from the food table.

I continued, "I was very afraid for a while. But I think I like being among the winners now. Something is bothering me, though. I don't think I will be the winner of the whole thing and I don't want to give up Master Kanoh's Iron Fist system when I lose." I felt a little nervous at speaking my rebellious thoughts out loud, but figured nobody, but Denju, would hear me in all the commotion.

With a mouth full of yogurt-dipped carrots, Denju said, much too loud for my comfort, "I'm not giving up the Tiger and Crane system of Master Kahl either!"

Then Han Erh spoke up from close behind us. "That's awfully impertinent talk from a man of seventeen, Denju."

I jumped forward, almost knocking Denju's precious bowl of food out of his hands, then whispered, "Good gain, Erh! Announce yourself first, will you?"

He smiled, then raised one eyebrow and said quietly, "I've spoken with most of my group; the ones you guys call *the showoffs*." He nodded at my sheepish blush and said, "It's all right, Jeng. We called you fellows *the shadows* last night because we were just as nervous about you sneaks as you were of us." Then he took hold of our tunics and drew us nearer to him while pretending to look over the food selections. He lowered his voice further and said, "I came to congratulate both of you, but more importantly to tell you to pass the word among your shadows that we showoffs all feel exactly what Denju just expressed…" he raised his eyebrows, "so loudly. As I said, please pass the word, but be discreet about it. You know how bad it could go if the Elders hear us openly dcfying them and their well-thought-out plan."

"What are you going to do?" I asked.

Han Erh shrugged and said, "That depends upon who wins." He walked away and disappeared into the crowd.

I spent the first hour of the break with Denju, spreading the word among the shadows. They all laughed at our group name and at the idea of the showoffs being afraid of us. Then my mother came and pulled me away. My cousins had many questions to ask me about war arts and the outside world. Most of their questions were irritatingly naïve. I smiled and answered them as courtesy demands, but avoided those questions I did not want to address. It seemed a very long time that I sat with my family. Then the Elders struck the town bell many times to get the tournament back in order. I was glad to get away from the interrogation, but some of the churning feeling returned to my stomach. I walked to the fighters' bench and sat down next to Denju, who had brought a full bowl of food with him.

"I talked to Han Erh," Denju said, not bothering to stop eating.

"About what?" I asked.

"About all the intrigue," he said, biting off half a baked yam and rolling it with his tongue to avoid getting burned. "He talked with Elder Korenda about the advantages offered by each style and how we should all teach each other."

"What did Elder say?"

"Bah! He wouldn't listen. Erh is just an unmarried boy in his eyes. The Elders barked so much about their all-wise and perfect plan while we were gone, that a change would make them look uninformed."

I said, "That's true, but…" I almost blurted out that Master Kanoh once said that Sanjurra's Elders know nothing, after he read their letter of introduction.

Denju continued eating and talking, "Erh said he offered them a way that would make the Elders look good while modifying their plan."

"What did they say to that?" I asked.

Denju stopped eating for a moment and said, "Korenda scolded Han Erh like a child in front of the other Elders and ordered him to never speak of his request again."

My cheeks suddenly became hot and the sound of my heartbeat rose in my ears. I wanted desperately to go and talk to Han Erh, but the Council was already walking onto the platform to resume the tournament. We waited perhaps a half hour for the Elders to get the crowd under control.

When all were relatively quiet, Elder Korenda drew a tile from his black bag and announced, "Chu Jeng of the Iron Fist system is the first fighter of this second round of eliminations."

Denju turned toward me and said with his mouth full, "Kick his butt out of the ring, Jeng."

I walked into the ring and made my sign of fealty.

Korenda drew a tile and announced my opponent. "The second fighter in this match will be Gar Jeng of the Coiling Serpent system."

I looked back at Denju, who sat stone still, no longer chewing the food in his full mouth. His eyes were wide, but he nodded and flashed me a good luck sign. The look in his eyes matched the feeling in my gut. I would rather be punched and kicked than choked and twisted to death. I backed to my edge of the ring as Gar Jeng confidently made his sign of fealty. When Korenda gave us the starting sign, we walked toward each other and stopped just out of striking distance.

"For the Coiling Serpent," Gar Jeng said very quietly, bowing his head slightly toward me.

"For the Iron Fist," I said, returning his salutation. Then I added, "All right, showoff. Let's see what you can do."

"Very well, shadow," he said with a slight smile. "I may let you walk in my shadow after this."

He assumed his twisted stance and immediately began his slithering advance. As I dropped into my best fighting horse I saw just how deceptive and frightening his movements were. Before I thought he was within striking range, he leapt forward and seized my forward guard, simultaneously winding his leg around mine. I punched at him with my rear hand, but he blocked it while trying to throw me down. The shocked look on his face told me that either he was used to throwing people down with ease or it hurt him to block my punch. At the time, I thought he was just shocked that he could not upset my horse, even though his wrist had felt soft and frail as it clashed against my own.

I knew I could not shake him off me and I did not want him to get his arms or legs tangled further with mine or wrapped around my neck or body. He twisted hard again to throw me down and it almost worked, but my stance was too deep and strong for that. I quickly decided to throw my hardest sweeping reverse knifehand strike toward his head. He barely blocked it in time. My arm nearly plowed its way through his arm to his head. He shouted out in pain and leaped away from me. He stood there blinking while I crescent-stepped toward him, feeling no pain at all. I remembered Master Kanoh telling me that all the grueling arm-bashing and herbal salve application we did would pay off in that way. Gar Jeng assumed his stance again. When I came within range, he swept his leg fast and low to knock my legs out from under me as I had seen the crane do earlier. His leg clashed against my horse and did nothing but cause me a little pain. In the next instant I lashed out with a forward hand punch to his sternum, followed immediately with the same hand rushing up his chest to thumb-strike him in the neck. He staggered back and fell to the ground with his eyes rolled up in his head, just as Master Kanoh said it would happen after such a punishing double waterfist strike.

Korenda pronounced me the victor to a cheering crowd. I think many people were quite astonished that the littlest of all the war artists had won two matches. I was becoming less astonished. Most of the fighters I had seen used terrible horse stances. They did not seem to know the tremendous importance of the horse. Doctor Li checked Gar Jeng and then lifted him to his feet after exchanging a few words with him.

When I sat down on the bench, Denju squeezed my leg with one hand. Bits of cornbread flew out of his mouth as he asked, "What do you have under those leggings, Armor?"

I laughed and said, "I just hope I don't have to fight you today." He returned to his dwindling food supply as the ring was raked in preparation of the priest's blessing and the next bout.

As soon as the ring was ready, Elder Korenda hushed the people and called out, "The fighters in this eleventh bout of the tournament are, Han Erh of the Southern Dragon system and Denju Rehn of the Tiger and Crane system."

Denju stood and belched quietly with his hand over his mouth. It seemed that as long as his belly was full, he was too satisfied to be worried about fighting Han Erh. The shadow and the showoff made their signs and faced each other in fighting stances. I could see right away that Han Erh's stance and guard were far superior to those of the younger man who stood a full head taller. They were both my friends, though they felt more like brothers to me. So I only hoped that neither of them would get hurt.

Denju Rehn and Han Erh fought hard and long. Denju used his superior strength to bat his lighter opponent around, but took many punishing blows himself. I had seen the dragon style artists take advantage of their opponents' more limited styles and expected the same in that fight. However, Denju was a tiger and crane stylist, which made him less predictable than the dragon would have liked. Soon both fighters were panting hard and bleeding from their noses and mouths. Erh's horse stance and guard still had most of their integrity, but the heavier man's form had seriously degenerated. Denju charged Erh and connected with a sweeping backfist to the dragon's head. Something looked wrong about it, in my eyes. Han Erh fell to the ground and started to get up immediately, but slowly. Denju rushed forward as if to strike the downed dragon. His guard was nonexistent. Just as he leaned over the dragon, Erh kicked upward with a thrusting knife edge kick to his lower ribs. With his body braced against the ground, his kick lifted the big man off his feet. Denju's legs crumpled beneath him when he landed, offering no resistance whatsoever. Erh stood up and waited, panting while the bear of a man rolled around and struggled to regain his feet.

Barely audible to the rest of us, Han Erh told Denju, "Don't get up, Brother."

The words did not seem to mean anything to Denju. He struggled to his feet and was still not breathing well at all. Han Erh did just what I thought I would try to do at that time. He hit Denju in the solar plexus before he regained his breath. That was all it took to end the fight. Denju staggered around for a short time, trying to catch his breath. Then his eyes rolled up and he took a few more steps forward with his hands out like a blind man. Han Erh caught him just before he would have fallen on the wooden beams of the ring. He let his friend down softly and helped Doctor Li to work at reviving him. Korenda declared Han Erh the winner. When Denju awoke, he was confused and tried to fight with Erh and the doctor. After six fighters struggled to hold him down and shout to him that the fight was over, he stopped and looked around blinking.

Denju's eyes met Erh's and he said, "I hope I don't look like you, but I feel worse."

"I don't know how you could!" Erh said. "I feel like I was swept under an avalanche of huge rocks!"

The entire crowd roared with laughter over Han Erh's play on the meaning of Denju's name. Both fighters walked with Doctor Li into Gener's store for treatment while men prepared the ring for the next fight. Noisy speculators hid the wagering table with their impatient crowding.

When the ring was ready, Korenda drew two tiles and announced, "The fighters of this twelfth fight of the competition are Tenju Gen of the White Dragon system and Kanu Rahn of the Eagle system." By the inflection of his voice I guessed that Korenda held a growing dislike for the White Dragon artist. The Elders did not tolerate anything which they thought threatened their authority. Most of the villagers agreed with them on that point. Elders were to be obeyed and young males without wives and children were nearly last in the traditional village power structure. To break the traditions of our fathers would not only be like abandoning one's parents to starvation; it would bring ghosts up from the netherworld and perhaps even demons down from the hills. Yet Tenju Gen refused to name his Master for the Elders. The Master's name was not important; the refusal was. I wondered what I would do if Master Kanoh had told me not to reveal his name. Despite my belief in tradition, I was coming to believe the Elders were too fixed and limited in their ways.

The grim-faced white dragon and the defiant eagle faced each other in the ring. Both moved with a fluid grace. Both reflected the spirit of their animal forms better than any of the others, except perhaps the two snakes. They had each watched the other in previous fights. Their slow advances and cautious testing each other out attested to their mutual respect. I could tell when the testing was done and the true fighting about to begin, because the eagle tightened up his guard and the dragon became perfectly still. He was strange to look at in his stillness. It seemed that there was something moving deep within him. I found my eyes jumping about as I tried to watch him steadily.

The eagle rushed the dragon in a circling attack, then faked a kick toward his leg. The kick immediately left its feigned path and flashed toward the dragon's face. He slipped his head just out of the kick's reach and countered with a quick shuffle forward and a series of twisted looping punches. The eagle dashed them all away and countered with a knifehand chop to the side of the dragon's neck. At first I thought the blow would have felled the dragon as it plowed deep into the target, driving the dragon nearly off his feet. But there was no sound of impact with the blow. The dragon had simply slipped along with the strike, rendering it useless. The strange event reminded me of, the old villager, Chang Euell, with his magic tricks and slight of hand illusions. Chang Euell was long dead by the time of the tournament, but I remembered his entertainments well from when he used to visit my father when I was a young child. Amazing as he was, I had never seen the old man perform such subtle tricks with his whole body as the dragon did. I found myself standing on my feet to watch, and I heard the rest of the fighters stand, some of them groaning with aches from previous fights.

Again and again, the dragon seemed to disappear from the power of his worthy opponent's blows while delivering punishing blows himself. Then the eagle fought his way in to dash the dragon's guard down and circle his arms inward like the flapping of an eagle's wings. His fierce knifehand chops were heading directly for the dragon's neck. There would be no slipping away from the opposing angles of the attack. Then the dragon dropped to the ground almost fast enough to avoid the blows that would have ended the bout. The eagle's chops crashed hard into the sides of the dragon's head, just above his temples. He was clearly dazed by the double blow. The eagle struck with his feet like talons as the dragon flopped around on the ground like a silken rag in the wind, avoiding nearly every blow. The eagle spent much of his time in the air, leaping over the dragon in desperate pursuit. It was like an eagle chasing a leaf in a whirlwind or trying to grasp a cloud in its talons. I watched their graceful dance in awe. Even as they grew fatigued, I stood spellbound by the perfection of their forms.

At length, the eagle backed off and let the dragon rise to his feet. I think he realized that the dragon was in his own element on the ground, riding the winds of battle like an eagle rides the winds of the sky. The two stood panting and staring at each other for quite some time before settling into their stances and advancing on each other again. Both had taken some hard blows, but neither of them could follow up their own successful attacks quickly enough to end the fight.

At length, the dragon rushed forward, leading his way in with dangerous kicks that the eagle was forced to avoid or block. He finished his complex attack with a driving punch to the eagle's chest. Before the eagle fell, his foot swept deceptively up into the dragon's groin. The dragon never saw it. He groaned and fell back like the eagle. After a considerable time lying separately on the ground, they stood up and faced off a third time. The crowd was pressing in around the ring, probably without realizing it. We fighters all pushed, pulled and wedged our way to the front. The fight was of particular interest to us. Besides, we could see and understand more in the fight than the untrained eyes of the villagers ever could.

The eagle tried to circle the dragon. For some reason, the dragon seemed to protect his sides and back less vigilantly than I would have. When it seemed the dragon was most vulnerable, the eagle leaped forward. His circular heel hook looked like it would fell a tree, but seemed to almost pass through the twisting dragon. Three more sharp kicks and punches found no hard mark on the white dragon who gave perfectly with each blow. Then in the midst of a wild flurry of exchanging blows, the eagle dropped to his knees. His arms hung limp at his sides and the dragon caught him before his face would have crashed to the ground. The crowd was silent.

Then Ben Jin, as if unable to contain himself anymore, shouted, "What was it? What felled him?"

"I think I saw a short uppercut." Han Erh said.

Tenju Gen was lowering his unconscious opponent to the ground as an ale-sodden villager shouted, "It was black magic what did it!"

Tenju Gen shot an angry glance at the man, who then stumbled backward, dousing his own face and chest with ale. "See what he did to me!" the man screeched. "He's a user of the evil arts!"

"You're tilted, Gwong! Shut up!" another man said after Gwong splashed ale on him too.

Cheng Ner must have sensed the danger to Tenju Gen as I did. My people greatly feared the black arts and did not tolerate those who dabbled in them. He shouted above the murmuring crowd, "I clearly saw a rising knee into Kanu Rahn's chest. It was a knee strike and nothing more!"

Arguments broke out as Doctor Li cautiously approached the fallen eagle, eying Tenju Gen with open suspicion.

Without even trying to hush the crowd, Korenda asked the white dragon, "Tenju Gen, are you a practitioner of the black arts of magic?"

Tenju Gen shook his head and narrowed his eyes. His lips had formed an angry thin line.

Korenda pressed him further, "Tell the Council of Elders the nature of your training and the name of your Master, before I declare you the winner in this bout."

The crowd hushed and Tenju Gen's voice could not mask his anger. "I cannot say more than that it was all physical. There was no magic at all."

Korenda brandished his authority carefully for all to see. "You will come before the Elders and explain your study to us."

"I will not," the dragon answered in a quiet cold voice.

The entire Council of Elders clambered to their feet. A gasp swept through the crowd, and Han Erh walked into the ring to stand by Tenju Gen's side. Senya Dain, the green dragon, joined him. The two snake stylists walked into the ring and stood defiant before the Council with the dragons. The rest of us war artists followed shortly thereafter. No more than twenty villagers joined us in the ring.

Senya Dain stepped forward and genuflected before Korenda and the other village fathers. He bowed his head low and spoke in the most courteous tones he could muster. "Good fathers, please declare this man the winner of the bout and let us get on with the service to our village that we have promised to render. My brothers and I will convince Tenju Gen to explain himself to you as you have so rightly requested. I beg your favor again, fathers. Let the tournament go on for the satisfaction of our wondering who will be village champion. Then question our brother Tenju Gen at your leisure."

With his head bowed low, Senya Dain did not see the angry shock on Korenda's face the first time he said "brothers" in reference to the war artists of the quest. The second mention of "brother" opened Korenda's mouth, but no words came out. His face was crimson with rage.

Senya Dain continued after a pause, "At least let our good village-fellows collect on their bets."

Cheers and nervous laughter rose up from the crowd. Korenda seemed to be struggling to control his rage. He turned toward his Council of Elders, most of whom nodded their agreement to the green dragon's request and the villagers' shouts.

"Remove all the kegs!" Korenda shouted, sweeping his pointed finger harshly across the crowd. "Tenju Gen is the winner of the fight!" He stormed off the platform and angrily supervised the removal of the kegs. I sat down on the bench with the rest of the fighters. I could not stop my hands from shaking. Few of us even whispered quietly to each other. I could feel the angry stares of some in the crowd behind me and hear their murmurs of shock and disappointment with us.

Korenda returned to the platform, grabbed two tiles from the bag and declared, "Amon Deng of the black tiger system and… Senya Dain will fight next."

Senya Dain made a quick finish of the black tiger, leading him to the edge of the ring, circling and kicking him out. Amon Deng first cursed himself, then laughed at the dragon's clever work. Not a blow was landed except for the kick that had sent him out of the ring, unharmed.

Korenda Pronounced Senya Dain the winner and the tournament stopped once again for those who were hungry. Korenda disappeared with his Council. Han Erh disappeared for a while too. Though the villagers remained somewhat festive, they began to shun the fighters as a group. I had a feeling that the rift between the men of the quest and Korenda was going to get worse very fast.

10 - FIRE

Korenda returned to the platform with his Council. Some of them were arguing with each other under their breaths. Korenda stood thin-lipped and stiff while the Elders sat down. He had only four tiles left in his bag; those of Senya Dain, Han Erh, Tenju Gen and my own tile. He drew two tiles at once. All ceremony had disappeared from his voice and manner. He said, "The next fight will be Tenju Gen against Han Erh." He clapped his hands and sat down without waiting for their signs of fealty.

The two fighters walked to the center of the ring together and genuflected before the Council. They backed away and assumed their stances. It did not seem to me, for a moment, that the dispute with Korenda had taken away their desire to fight and win. They launched at each other with all the graceful fury of colliding cyclones. Han Erh was on the attack most of the time, while the white dragon slipped and disappeared from most of his blows. It was almost like watching a man fight with his own shadow or like watching a child trying to take hold of his reflection in water. Han Erh's southern dragon offense was frightening to watch. The white dragon was equally intimidating to see in action. Several times the white dragon trapped the arms of the southern dragon for brief instants to show that he could have broken them. But he did this only after the southern dragon showed him many times that he could have killed or blinded him if his own techniques were not forbidden in the tournament.

The dragons were both tiring when Han Erh took hold of both Tenju Gen's wrists. Erh spun his body and yanked the white dragon's arms around in a great high to low circle. The white dragon sailed head over heels and crashed to the ground. He arose and stood unharmed, but backed away from Han Erh and genuflected to him, recognizing him as the superior fighter.

The significance of the white dragon's sign of fealty was not lost on Korenda. He stood and shouted with fists clenched at his sides, "Tenju Gen is defeated!"

The wagering table paid off its bets and raked in losses. When the crowd of gamblers left the table, it was laden with money stacked on the names of the three remaining fighters. I heard villagers talk of the dragons being superior to all the rest of the fighters. I forgave them their ignorance. After all, there were the legends of great dragons living as guardians of man and hiding in deep waters, high mountains or even in the clouds and other mysterious places. Almost everyone believed in dragons, though nobody who cared about their credibility ever claimed to have actually seen one.

As soon as the ring was cleared, Korenda drew the only two tiles from the bag and read the names of Senya Dain and Chu Jeng. I stood and walked into the ring with the green dragon.

As we made our signs to the Elders, the green dragon whispered, "Yield quickly, boy, and I won't hurt you."

I looked directly at him and said, "Cower on your back now and I won't hurt *you!*" He did not laugh and I did not mean it as a joke. I suppose he had not meant to insult me, but his words had felt like an insult. At that instant I decided the proud dragons would recognize the Iron Fist of Kanoh Feng and respect it.

I backed away from the dragon and formed a flat horse. He looked at me strangely and formed a fine looking fighting horse stance. It seemed to me that his guard was a little too low, So I shuffled closer and when in range, I struck toward his head. He raised his guard just as I thought he would. I took advantage of his defense and swept my shin through the back of his forward leg. He hit the ground hard on his back though his fall was expertly controlled. When he came to his feet, he could not hide the pain in his calf.

I delivered the same attack with twice the speed, catching him on the shin with my shin. He fell to the ground and again expertly broke his hard fall. His pain seemed twice as bad as before when he clambered to his feet. I began the same attack again and saw the dragon wince in pain and jump to avoid the sweep. But I changed the attack in the middle, raising my sweep to catch his ribs and forward guard with my shin. He toppled backward and almost landed on his neck. I had listened to my Master's stories of war and strategy. He had called that pattern of attack a triple gate and it worked well against the green dragon. Senya Dain backed away and looked at me with wide eyes. I guessed that I had gained his respect.

It was then that I realized I had a chance to win the tournament. I thought my dream might come true at last! I was just about to launch myself forward into an attack, when the dragon attacked first. He must have seen my eyes light up. Master had always said I hide the weather of my mind like the open sky hides a coming storm. The dragon stifled me and punched my nose hard. He followed his punch with a lightning fast wheel kick to my sternum. I felt my heart pounding in my neck as blood spurted from my nose. My eyes watered and blurred. He followed his attack quickly with another kick toward my head. I blocked it with the outer bone of my forearm. He groaned in pain and jumped back. A dark red stain spread out on the shin area of his leggings. I blocked several strikes of his next complex attack as hard as I could. I imagined his limbs were sticks thrown at me by Master Kanoh. I knew I was hurting him, but many of his strikes got through and hurt me right back. He took my breath and made my head dizzy. I could taste blood. I even had to spit some of it out to keep from choking. My torn lips felt foreign to my tongue. Then I noticed my arms were covered in blood that was not my own. The dragon's shins and arms were cut in many places. I had to end the fight before neither of us could continue on to fight Han Erh.

I took my Master's advice and attacked the dragon while he was tired. I was not the least tired of breath or leg, though I was weary of being hit. I attacked him and did not let up when it seemed natural to do so. The dragon became visibly desperate to disengage from the flurry, but still I did not let up. I pursued him until his desperation and fatigue made him sloppy. Then I hammered my fists repeatedly down on his head as he faltered. At last he sprawled out on the ground and did not get up for a long time. Only when he fell, did I realize that much of the crowd had been chanting, "Chu Jeng! Chu Jeng! Chu Jeng!" as we fought. I have never felt prouder, before or since.

Elder Korenda allowed me a three-hour rest, to recover before fighting Han Erh. I refused to let Doctor Li treat my wounds until he was completely finished with Senya Dain. My mother and father led me into Gener's store and tried to stop the bleeding of my nose until the doctor came to me.

The doctor examined the contusions on my legs and arms after he worked on my nose and stopped the flow. He squinted and sucked air through his teeth. "Foolish boy, you are going to feel these for weeks to come!"

"I didn't fight like a boy. Did I, Father?"

"No, son," my father replied, unable to hide the mix of pride and sorrow in his voice. "You fought like ten tigers!"

"Master used to put a salve on my bruises that… Oh! I forgot what he gave me! Mother, please run home and get me a small gray jar, sealed with bee's wax. I have it hidden in the bottom of my trunk. Please. It contains something that will help me today! Oh. How could I have forgotten it? It is the potion Master gave me to take before the tournament."

Mother dashed off without a word.

"What is in it?" the doctor asked.

"I have no idea," I replied, to his obvious disappointment.

Just then Korenda walked into the store and squatted near me. "I pray that you win, son," he said solemnly.

I tried to stand up for my Elder, but the doctor put his hand on my chest and shook his head.

Korenda continued, "May Heaven bless you with strength and faithfulness. The village depends on you alone, Chu Jeng." Turning to my parents, he said, "You have a son to be proud of. He knows his place in service to our village and there is no element of insubordination in him."

My father frowned slightly and I felt there was more warning in the Elder's words than praise.

The doctor finished his work and left me in my father's care. When My mother returned with the potion, I removed the seal and drank it all down. It tasted horrible as did all the Master's potions. Soon I began to feel the familiar tingling feeling of his rooty concoctions. That time, though, the tingling sensation did not stop increasing until I thought I must stand or burst. I struggled to my feet and walked quickly around the room. The sound of my feet on the wooden floor seemed unnaturally loud to me, and it seemed that my injuries had completely healed. Looking at my forearm, I saw the grisly evidence of my mistaken notion.

I turned toward my father and said, "I'm ready to fight." Then I raised my fists and shouted, "By Heaven, I feel great!"

"Let me help you to feel even greater, Jeng," he said. "I have been betting on you all along and have won a full three years wages already. At your mother's request, I have hidden half of the money under the house and am betting the other half on you to defeat Han Erh."

"What are the odds against me?" I asked.

"Better than when you started today."

"But what, exactly?"

"Twenty-three to one against you."

At first I was disappointed at the low opinion the villagers held of me. Then I realized that they were judging by appearances and by Han Erh's awesome, long-standing reputation. "I think I can beat him," I said at last.

My father smiled, raised his eyebrows and said, "You have the fire, Jeng. Show him your Iron Fist."

"Don't toy with him like you did with Senya Dain," my mother said. "If you take a beating like that again, I will run in there and stop the fight

78

myself. I swear, Jeng!"

"Heaven's gain, Mother! I wasn't toying with him. I fought as hard as I could." I shook my head and forced myself not to look at her with a disrespectful expression.

Her voice wavered as she looked deeply into my eyes and said, "Jeng, your eyes have changed. You seem so different since you came back from the outside world. I don't feel I quite know you as I once did."

My father took her hand and squeezed it, saying, "He is the same as ever, woman, just more grown up." His tone was full of uncertainty, though. I think neither of them felt they knew me anymore. In truth, they could not have understood what I had been through, or what any of my brothers had been through.

The time for the fight arrived and the village bell pealed out like a warning. I made my way to the ring, which was crowded to its edge by excited villagers. I appeared in the ring just after Han Erh. The crowd cheered for me as it had for him. It seemed that the spectators were split in half along the edges of the fighting ring. Han Erh's showoffs were on the eastern side and most of my shadows stood along the west. Most of my relatives stood with the shadows. Then I saw Denju Rehn leading my mother and father to the ringside with the rest of the shadows.

Elder Korenda strained to be seen over the throng. The ceremony had returned to his voice as he said, "The final bout of the Sanjurra Village War Art Championship is between Han Erh of the Southern Dragon system and the worthy and respectful Chu Jeng of the Iron Fist system." After we made our signs of fealty, he clapped his hands, nodded and smiled directly at me.

The shadows and showoffs began to alternately chant against each other, "Chu Jeng! Han Erh! Chu Jeng! Han Erh!"

Erh and I circled each other watchfully and then settled into our horses. I still felt great with Master Kanoh's potion running its energetic way through my veins. I launched a fast leaping side thrust kick at Erh. He partially blocked it with one forearm, but it threw him back and sent him staggering toward the pressing, cheering crowd. I realized then that there would be no win by driving my opponent out of the ring. I rushed him and threw a sweeping backfist and a hooking punch as he staggered backward. He blocked both of them, gritting his teeth with pain as his wrists clashed against mine. The crowd shouted our names louder and Erh tried the sweeping Iron Broom technique on my forward leg. It only pushed my foot about three inches backward and Erh nearly fell forward to the

79

ground. His right side was exposed to me as he reached down with his right hand to stop is fall. I instantly punched him in the back of the head, but he appeared to have felt it coming and gave with it expertly. I followed my unsuccessful punch with a shin kick to his open ribs. He pulled his right upper arm back just in time to partially block the kick. Even with the partial block, Erh grunted as his wind was taken from him. He rolled to his side, but kept a guard up with both his hands and feet. I knew better than to attack a dragon who waited on the ground for me. I backed up and Erh waited for his breathing to return before standing up in his horse.

The dragon stifled my next three attacks, but his arms were bleeding from clashing against my strikes. Then he rushed me; whirling fists and kicks lashing out like a maelstrom of fury. His attacks broke against my defense like a wave against rocks. I countered his attack immediately and violently. His long legs carried him quickly out of my reach as he put up a desperate defense. Many hands came out from the crowd and stopped him from inadvertently stepping out of the ring. He stood in his failing horse stance and panted close to the edge of the crowd. His shoulders drooped and his guard appeared to be much more defensive than dangerous. His face had lost most of its color. I inched closer to him while he was so weak and afraid. I would make my next attack the one that ended it all. Suddenly Erh leapt toward me with his forward fist flying toward my head. I did not have time to blink before I saw a bright flash of searing white light and felt my head vaulting backward. I struggled to keep my feet as everything went black. I felt gentle hands on my back, letting me down to rest on the ground. I wanted to rest.

I awoke to the sound of a crowd triumphantly chanting, "Han Erh! Han Erh! Han Erh!" I also heard my mother quietly crying and Doctor Li asking me, "What is your name, son?"

I could not see him in the darkness. "What part of the day is it?" I asked.

"Can you tell me your name, young man?" he asked, gently padding my forehead with a cold wet cloth.

"I'm… Is it after nightfall?"

My mother gasped and held her breath.

"Mother?" I asked. "That is you, isn't it?"

Doctor Li cautioned her, "Let him say his own name first."

I could begin to see the outline of his face against a dark gray sky.

"I'm here, son," Mother said.

Her voice was as sweet as honey to my ears. I reached out to her and she grasped my hand, squeezing it tightly. I realized then that I must have hurt my hand in the fight. I thought it was Han Erh but could not be sure.

"I can see a little, now."

Mother squeezed my hand harder and choked.

The sky brightened more and I said, "Doctor Li, my name is Chu Jeng of the Iron Fist."

"Likewise of the iron skull," he said with a sigh. "Now how many fingers am I holding up?"

"Five and a half," I answered, seeing that one of them was bent at the second knuckle. The sky had become a bright blue with a few fluffy white clouds. "How long was I down?" I asked.

"About a quarter hour," the doctor said, gathering his things. Then turning to my parents, he said, "You better walk with him so that he doesn't fall. I don't want that cut opening up again."

My hand involuntarily rose to a thick bandage on my head where I remembered being hit before I fell.

"No, no, no!" Doctor Li said. "Nobody touches that but me. When it is healed—only when it is healed—then it is your head again! I suggest you find more sensible things to do with it from now on, young man. And now I'll bid a good day to you all. I'm tired."

Father helped me to my feet. I started forward between him and my mother. My knees felt wobbly and my head began to throb with an amazing pain.

From close behind me I heard Kanu Rahn say, "Please forgive us, Chu Benya."

I turned to see all the shadows assembled behind me, beaming with pride. "Forgive us, Mrs. Chu," he continued, "but you simply cannot deprive us of our hero. Chu Jeng is Lord of the Shadows! I am afraid these fine men will riot if they cannot carry him on their shoulders before the crowd."

They lifted me to their shoulders and Denju Rehn called back to my parents, "We will take good care of him. You have my promise!"

The chant of "Chu Jeng! Chu Jeng! Chu Jeng!" rose to compete with Han Erh's adulation. My chant never rose as loud as his though, which I felt was appropriate since I lost the final bout. But, oh! I felt like a winner.

For the first time in my life, I was a winner, a champion rather than the skinny boy who could not do it.

A mug of cool foamy ale made its way from hand to hand and into my own. Denju laughed and exclaimed, "You earned it, Brother. You bettered every man, but Erh."

Then lanky Kor Den shouted, "Any man who calls my brother a boy will face the fury of the Mountain Crane!"

"That's if the Coiling Serpent is kind enough to leave anything of him for you!" Gar Jeng countered.

"The Praying Mantis will get him first," Torin Feng shouted.

All the shadows took a turn shouting praises of their individual systems. They carried me round the market circle amid the cheering crowd. Han Erh bounced along on his showoffs' shoulders opposite me. We waved to each other, then the town bell began to ring. It took the Elders nearly an hour to stop all the feasting, drinking, cheering and reveling. In time, Han Erh stood alone in the fighting ring before the stern-faced Elders and a hushed crowd.

11 - CONFEDERACY

The air pressed in upon me with an ugly tension as rumors of an angry Council spread quickly through the gathering crowd. One day earlier I would have been terrified by what I felt. But I was so confident in that I had been tested in the fire of the day and come out strong. Besides, my sixteen strong Brothers of the Quest were with me. Except for Han Erh, who stood in the middle, the war artists all stood together at the edge of the ring. Though the villagers pressed their way in close to the action, they stood a cautious arm's length from us. Our family members even stood away from us as if they suspected we were about to burst into flame at any moment. My eyes searched until they met my mother's gaze. I felt that she was torn between love and fear. Father stood with her, his eyes glued to Elder Korenda.

Korenda, the head of the Council of Elders, spoke with a mix of ceremony and fear. His eyes scanned the crowd as he said, "So much of our resources, thoughts, prayers and efforts have gone into this day. I commend the good people of Sanjurra for the result of their efforts." He gestured toward Han Erh. Then he directed his most stern gaze on the lone war artist. "Han Erh, it is the will of this Council and the expectation of the villagers that you keep your word as winner of the contest. You were called by fate to be champion of Sanjurra. You shall teach your Southern Dragon war art to the others, who shall forget their arts as all agreed, one year ago."

I felt anger well up in me and my aching head throbbed more painfully. A wave of quiet, irate murmurs ran through the body of war artists.

Han Erh seemed to be struggling with his next words. At last he said, "My good Elders, I submit to your wise counsel that each of these brave fighters has skills that I do not. It would be a waste, in my humble opinion, to throw such knowledge away before we test it for its possible use in defense of the village."

Korenda could not contain his anger. "You have been warned this day against such insolence, boy!"

The head Elder's reference to Han Erh as a boy caused my mouth to fly open in angry shock. Senya Dain stomped his foot and Tenju Gen said, just loud enough for Erh and a few others to hear, "That changes the rule, Han Erh. Spread your wings!"

Erh stiffened up and said, "I would not have defied your ill-advised plan in public if you had taken my advice in private, Korenda. I will keep my service to the village, more effectively than you perhaps, but I will not throw away wheat as if it were chaff, just because you ignorantly call it chaff."

Korenda stood with his fists shaking at his sides and screamed, "Chu Jeng is declared champion of Sanjurra! His Iron Fist style will be our village defense. All other arts will be forgotten."

There was only one thing I could do. I could see that Korenda felt his power was threatened. He was backed into a self-made trap, made worse by his own ignorance and inflexibility. I knew how all the others felt. So I walked to the fighting ring next to Han Erh and said, "I stand with my brother, Han Erh, in the best service to our village that I can give."

Korenda's voice was utterly out of control as he screeched, "You are both declared outlaw!" Declaring anyone outlaw was a right and power that he must have known, in more lucid moments, that he did not have. "Who will come forward to remove these hooligans from our village circle?"

The two dragon stylists, Senya Dain and Tenju Gen, came forward to stand at our sides. The snake stylists followed soon thereafter. At last, all seventeen fighters stood together in the fighting ring. The villagers backed farther away from us.

Korenda groaned as if in pain and stumbled backward with the color drained from his face. He staggered off the platform as if drunk and fled toward his home. The Elders followed him in angry silence. I never felt more uncomfortable in my life. The crowd began to quietly drift off, eventually leaving us alone in the fighting ring. None of us knew quite what to do.

Tenju Gen was the first to speak up. "Han Erh, I meant it when I gave my sign of fealty to you this day. It is all the more righteous now, since you are our leader by right of conquest."

Senya Dain said, "I will reaffirm my fealty to you now, Han Erh." He stepped out in front of us to face his chosen leader and genuflect.

"No!" Han Erh said abruptly. Then he gathered us close and spoke quietly. "If you feel that way, then please do not show it to those who would not understand and might assume treason. The moon will be full in three days. I will meet you and all who wish to come to *our* council at the forest clearing west of the late Chu Senji's pond. I will be waiting in darkness at the third hour of the full moon. Now go home to your families. I think we all know what not to say if questioned." After his last words, he held our eyes individually until we each nodded our assent.

We quietly drifted off in our own directions, but I waited until long after dark to go home. When I arrived at the family farm, I stared at my house in the moonlight. The stars glittered brightly in the sullen sky. Candles shone from the windows of the farmhouse. Mother and Father were waiting for me. On a hunch, I walked back south toward town. When I reached the crossroads, I did not turn west toward the village, but continued south and walked another three-and-a-half miles to Senya Dain's house. I knocked on his door. Han Erh answered. He let me in and I saw Amon Deng and Gar Jeng sitting at Senya Dain's table.

Dain arose from the table and said, "Join us, Jeng. We were all too unnerved to sleep yet tonight."

"I'm not," I answered. "It's just that my parents are waiting up for me and I don't want to talk right now. I want to sleep. I thought I might ask you if I could stay here for the night."

Dain laughed and said, "You certainly may, Jeng." He made me a pallet of blankets and a pillow of clean, rolled up clothes. I remember lying down, and hearing a few polite words from my fellow war artists bidding me a good night. Dreams of a safe haven I had once found with the Bright Moon Society followed immediately.

I awoke the next morning to Senya Dain's call. "Chu Jeng. Get yourself up. I have breakfast ready. You need good food to heal those wounds."

I sat up and my throbbing head agreed with Dain that I had some healing to do. "I had a good dream," I said to him. "Do you want to hear about it?"

"No," he replied with a dry smile. "Do you want to eat?"

"Yes, thank you." I stood up and stretched painfully, then added, "Where are the others?"

"They've already eaten and are tending my ducks while discussing the tournament." Then he laughed and said, with comically wide eyes, "I still can't believe I was beaten by a scrawny little boy!" He noticed my reaction and added with a smile, "I apologize, Jeng. You are no boy by any measure, but years."

He served me fried duck eggs, carrots, rice and rose-petal tea. It was an odd breakfast for me, but I ate it as if starved, especially the eggs. When I had taken my fill, Dain sat down and ate with surprisingly coarse manners. Then I remembered that he had lived for too long without the refining company of a woman. He lived without anyone and was obviously used to eating alone. But, despite his years of solitude, he seemed quite comfortable eating with one of his outcast fellow war artists at his table.

85

As he finished his morning meal and stood up from the table, I asked, "What are we going to do, Dain?"

"I don't know," he answered. "I have certain things I want to do, but I suppose it's mostly up to Han Erh. He's our rightful leader. As I think of it, Jeng. You were almost our leader. You were running Erh out of the ring, but the press of the crowd kept him in. If not for their many hands against his back, you would have won. Unbelievable!" He shook his head, then said, "But true nonetheless. Do you feel cheated?"

I had already thought about what he mentioned, and had come to a peaceful agreement with it before I reached his house the night before. "No. I don't feel cheated. Erh is our rightful leader. Though I could defeat any one of you, I don't have Erh's qualities. I think we all look up to him. It is best this way. Please don't ever mention your observation to the others."

He nodded and said, "There is still the problem of Elder Korenda declaring that you and Erh are outlaws."

"He can't do that without the consent of the whole Council," I replied.

"But will the Council defy him in this matter or support him? You two hang in the balance here until they make their decision. I think it could likely happen either way."

I stayed at Senya Dain's house until Han Erh's council of the full moon. Han Erh stayed with us and the fighters all agreed to tell no villager of our whereabouts. On the night before the night of the full moon, word came to us that the Council had overturned Korenda's condemnation of Erh and me. They had, however, debated long on the subject and publicly expressed extreme displeasure with the whole of the warriors. Many of the war artists came to give their advice to Han Erh before he held his council. He listened to them all, but firmly refused to tell any what his mind held.

Half of the fighters congregated at Senya Dain's house on the night of the full moon. We walked to the forest clearing at the appointed time and met the remainder of our number waiting for us there. Erh walked in silence onto a small knoll near the north end of the moonlit glade. A cool spring breeze wafted the tall grass in whispering waves around us. The looks on the faces of my compatriots suddenly reminded me of my friends in the Bright Moon Society. I felt very much at home in the company of these men. I barely restrained a sudden urge to shout a vow of brotherhood with them for the moon and stars to witness.

Han Erh began his council in this way, "My Brothers, we are each incomplete in our arts and must combine them into one system. Before we start, I invite any man here to leave now if he feels he has nothing to offer to the rest of us." Erh waited for a response from any who would leave, then continued, "I also invite any who desire to side with the Council to leave now. The Council would surely declare him champion and lavish him with public honor. Furthermore, I would not dare to criticize any man for making such a choice."

His last invitation drew a barrage of angry invective directed at the Council and especially at Elder Korenda.

Han Erh silenced us and said, "As angry with the Council as we are, we must not let anger provide our purpose or rule our existence. One year ago, I set my feet upon a quest of service to justice and liberation of our people from the oppression of banditry. You joined me in that quest and I believe you are here tonight, not only because the Council stands against you, but because you are faithful to our quest and stand strong for the safety and freedom of our people." Han Erh smiled at our nods of agreement. He continued, "We will all take our turns guarding this place by threes each night at sundown. This will be our secret domain in which to practice our arts. Each of us will refine and catalog his art to add to the rest when we're ready. The time of our birth as a society of defenders has come. Diversity is our unpredictable way because of our many skills and strategies. I feel the dawning of a new age of fighting art because we will unite our skills in secret to form a fighting system that is second to none!"

We barely restrained our cheering to a dull roar. I found myself jumping and raising my fist in the air as if punching the old demons of doubt and fear away. Han Erh stepped from his knoll to walk among us. We crowded around him and began to ask him questions all at once.

Erh raised his forefinger, paused and pointed toward the edge of the clearing. "That area is mine, for now," he said as he started to walk away from us. Without turning back he said, "Trou Gom, Gis Erh and Rume Lak have the first guard. Into the forest with you and keep any strangers away while the rest of us practice!"

I chose a good flat area of grass and began to practice my basic punches, kicks and blocks from a flat horse stance. I ignored the other thirteen fighters practicing in the glade around me. I worked for hours in the glade that night and tried to make my efforts an example to all my brothers. I was the most reluctant to leave when we decided to quit for the night. I returned home and struggled carefully to sneak into the house without my parents noticing.

I made it almost to my bed when Father came into my room behind me and said, "Son, how could you do this to your mother?"

I nearly jumped out of my shoes at the first sound of his voice. I had expected more anger, but the quiet disappointment in his voice was bad enough. I turned to look at him and did not know what to say. I was ashamed about the outcome of the tournament as it must have appeared in his eyes. Yet I was elated about the development of other things that I was forbidden to tell him. I also knew that I could never explain them in a way that he could understand, wise though he was.

"She weeps into her pillow even now," he added.

My gut twisted inside as I bowed low and said, "I am terribly sorry, Father. You know how I…"

"I know," he said quietly. "But you are her only child and you know how a mother must worry for her own."

In my mind, I saw her crying in silence. "What should I do?" I asked him in a whisper as I fought back my tears.

He thought for a while and said, "Do for her what your heart tells you in the morning. Never again leave us like this without sending word. How you could ever be so cold-mannered and careless I cannot understand." He stood in silence for a while, then said, "How is your head?"

"It is getting better, I think."

He turned and began to walk back to his room. Then he stopped and said loud enough for my mother to hear, "Eat something before you sleep." In a whisper he added, "I thank Heaven that you are home and safe, son."

The next night I returned to the clearing, just after sundown. I had guard duty that night and I slithered through the shadows like a snake, watching for strangers. I circled the clearing randomly from left to right and back again. I thought of several ways I would turn any stranger away. Perhaps I could try to frighten them away by growling from the concealment of the undergrowth. Or I could tell them that I was sent to find them by a family member who needed them. While I stalked the woods in silence, I came up with many plans to dissuade any intruder from approaching our secret domain. I dripped with sweat from the unfamiliar exertion of moving silently and from a slight nervousness inherent to the hunt.

Suddenly I felt a deliberate tap on my right shoulder. I involuntarily grunted aloud and whirled around, snapping the stick that was touching my shoulder in half with the edge of my wrist. Before I could stop myself, I instantly lashed out with a kick at Gar Jeng. Luckily, he was just out of my range.

Gar Jeng fell to the ground, laughing as quietly as he could. He rolled and held his stomach, unable to speak through his laughter. I began quietly throwing handfuls of dirt and forest litter at him, until I joined him laughing and panting on the ground.

"You creepy, slimy snake!" I whispered at him. "How long have you been following me?"

Between laughter-racked pants of breath he said, "Chu Jeng, your face was so funny! I didn't know eyeballs could get that big!"

Indignantly, I said, "I saw you a couple of times earlier, but I didn't try to sneak up on you!"

"You can't sneak up on a snake, Jeng," he replied.

That proud statement was the inauguration of the sneaking, stalking game that we played every night from then on. Every war artist among us honed his stalking, hiding and avoiding skills as well as patterns of speech to confuse and dissuade any intruder. We soon recognized Onde Tor, Rume Lak and Ben Jin as the masters of deceptive speech. We acknowledged Denju Rehn, Amon Deng and Gis Erh as masters of the sudden unexpected attack. Cheng Ner, Trou Gom and Gar Jeng crept about with the greatest shadowy silence. The three dragons; Han Erh, Senya Dain and Tenju Gen proved to be the most unpredictable in their patterns of deception. But the true master of the night was the white dragon stylist, Tenju Gen. We came to call him the Forest Mist; for he could not be found or touched. Just when one of us thought he had Tenju Gen in front of him, the dragon would maneuver like a silent mist through the trees and tap the stalker's shoulder from behind. Several times he was able to tap his opponent and disappear without a trace. It was eerily unnerving to go up against him in the dark woods around the clearing.

Onde Tor was the grandmaster of mystical speech among us. He had learned enough from his Master to be able to make most of the rest of us do things we had not intended. He could talk to us in a calm, even manner that would make us relax our guards. He could even talk most of us down into sleep, even if we were not the least tired. He could wind his words together with our feelings and make us believe almost anything, even if we knew he was trying to do it. Luckily for us he never used his skill against us in any sort of bad way. After some persuasion from Han Erh, Onde Tor began teaching us how to use his powerful patterns of speech. He said that teaching us helped him to understand more deeply, exactly what it was he was doing.

Other than comparing and refining our methods of stalking, hiding and speaking persuasively, we exchanged no arts with each other. Instead, we perfected our own arts. Those who studied the animal arts immersed themselves in the spirits of their animals. Amon Deng became more tiger-like in his attitude, movements and even in his walk. Torin Feng became weirdly mantis-like in everything he did. He even stalked wild birds like a mantis stalking a fly. One day he brought us a freshly killed dove he claimed to have snatched from the air as it flew past him.

"What made it fly so close to you?" Han Erh asked him.

Torin Feng looked astonished at our leader's ignorance. "I made myself look like a branch! How else?"

Those who had studied weapons, carved practice swords, spears, canes and staves from the trees of the forest. Kor Den purchased a chain, which he whirled around himself with deadly speed and accuracy. Senya Dain had the village blacksmith form him some darts and razor-edge coins, which he could embed deeply into the trunks of trees from a long distance. He fashioned a leather sling and practiced with it in the glade, much to our amazement. I had never before seen anyone use a sling the way he did. He made the sling seem like a whole different weapon and I gained new respect for what was commonly looked upon as a child's toy.

We practiced in secret for all the summer months and well into autumn. It was not long before we had packed all the grass down with our feet during our practice sessions. Eventually we wore the ground to bare, loose dirt. I thought Master Kanoh would have been proud of us if he could have seen the way we pushed ourselves toward excellence. We dug a secret pit with a concealed lid at the edge of the forest. In the pit we lowered a trunk sealed against water with pitch on the outside. It held the papers on which we were cataloging our fighting systems. Our lives went on fairly normally in the village and it was altogether a peaceful time of motivation and easy brotherhood. The elders never mentioned the quest or competition again, and the villagers rarely discussed it in audible tones, and never when the elders were within earshot. For the daily life of the village, it was as if we had never returned from the outside world. And, as far as the closeness we once had with our neighbors and friends in Sanjurra, it was as if we never should have returned.

As the end of autumn and the harvest approached, we had all finished preparing our arts for convergence into a single combined fighting system. We began to discuss and sometimes argue about how to combine them. Everyone wanted his own fighting art to bear the strongest mark on the new system. Our disagreements soundly prevented the beginning of the process.

12 - BANISHMENT

Early in the damp cool of night, I took my watch along with Denju Rehn and Torin Feng. I was stalking Denju and just about had him in a vulnerable position. He was easy to stalk and follow because of his large relatively ungraceful form, but he was always on guard against attack. The final approach would be difficult. I breathed as silently as I could while taking extremely slow steps, listening for the slightest crackle of forest litter beneath my feet. I could hear my compatriots practicing in the clearing off to my left. I hoped that even their hushed work would cover up my own quiet movements. Then I heard someone trying very unsuccessfully to sneak up toward me from my right. I thought Torin Feng must be getting slow in the head to move so clumsily, or perhaps, that he was acting clumsy as a joke. Denju Rehn must have heard it too; for he crouched low and began carefully wending his way toward the sound. I heard a slight cough from the direction of the approaching footsteps and knew instantly that it was not Torin Feng. It was an intruder sneaking up on our secret place!

My heart began to pound as my mind raced for a solution to the problem. I had been so intent on Denju Rehn and the stalking game that the unexpected threat of real danger left me dumbfounded. The intruder was approaching very fast; putting more effort into speed than into stealth. Before I could think of anything sensible to do, he came upon me. I could not let him pass me and find the rest of the war artists in the clearing, doing just what the Council of Elders had forbidden us from doing. He did not see me crouched in the undergrowth. Without thinking of the consequences, I lashed out with my shin against his. He screamed with surprise and pain before falling like a rock. Denju crashed toward us through the leafy growth. I delivered a bear paw slap to the stranger's head, then another. He moved slightly and I struck him again.

Then Denju tackled me from the side and said, "Stop it, Jeng! You're killing him!"

I was suddenly every bit as terrified at my own lack of self control as I was of the stranger discovering us. The sweet odor of blood mixed with that of my own nervous perspiration. Soon the whole body of war artists crowded around Denju, the downed stranger and me.

Erh spoke up first, asking, "Is he alive?"

I groped for the stranger's chest until I felt a heartbeat. "Yes," I answered. "I'm sorry, Erh. I panicked."

Without looking away from the stranger's body, Erh said, "Get the trunk of papers out of here. Ben Jin, Gar Jeng, Rume Lak and Trou Gom, carry it to Senya Dain's house. Avoid the roads and the village. Senya Dain and Tenju Gen, guard them as they move. This clearing is no longer ours."

Denju Rehn lifted the stranger's head and brushed dirt off his face as he asked, "What will we do with him? We can't leave him here in the darkness of the forest where he will get no help."

Han Erh thought for a moment and said to Denju, "You will help Chu Jeng and me to take him to the market circle and ring the bell. We will disappear quickly and pray that he doesn't die before Doctor Li can help him. The rest of you get back to your homes immediately. You had better be in your beds before we ring the bell. Go now!"

As soon as we came into the moonlight on the open road, we saw that the wounded stranger was Chen Bin. Skinny Chen was one of Gener Chig's fawning toadies and Gener Chig was Han Erh's only enemy.

Erh looked at Chen Bin's face for a few moments and said, "There is only one reason he would be sneaking toward the clearing so late at night. Gener Chig knows something goes on here."

"How?" I asked as we carried the young man toward town.

Erh answered, "Gener Chig is always probing into affairs that are not his own. He likes best to use his power where it is most inappropriate. And this is how he likes to do it; by paying others to risk themselves for his selfish whims."

Then I felt even worse for having hurt Chen Bin. I had never liked the shifty-eyed little rat, but the thought of him being seriously injured for a few of Gener Chig's coppers was an injustice. And I had taken part in that injustice. Even worse was that Gener Chig was hunting for a way to weaken Han Erh's influence over Han Rinya's parents. He was now closer to achieving his goal.

We gently laid Chen Bin on the ground of the market circle and Erh said, "Run home, Jeng. And don't fret. You did nothing wrong."

His voice was laden with worry and his words did nothing to console me. I ran home and snuck back into bed, but did not sleep. In the morning, when my father called me to help him work, I was sweating, shaking and chilled with nerves. My mother insisted I stay in bed, thinking I was sick. I did not leave the farm for several days, even though I recovered from my mysterious *illness* and went to work.

Then my Aunt Ninya came to visit. I overheard her telling my mother, "I have terrible news." She always relished the opportunity to pass on terrible news, especially if it was none of her concern. "Poor Chen Bin was lured from his home by black magic and brutally attacked several nights ago."

"Heaven protect us!" my mother said, accepting her sister's preposterous gossip without raising a single question.

"Oh, yes," Aunt Ninya continued. "Some say it was one of the young war artists that returned to us from the outside world with strange ways and defiant tempers."

"Jeng came back to his father and me with no strange ways or defiant temper," my mother countered with less confidence in her voice than I would have liked to hear.

"Just you beware, Sister. They are all better at hiding it than you and I are at detecting it. Who does your young Jeng group with, but the others of his kind? Hmm? Some say they go out at night like vampires and talk with demons in the forest."

"That's ridiculous," my mother insisted. "My Jeng wouldn't speak with a demon to save his own two legs. I don't think any ill of the other young war artists either. Chen Bin was probably attacked by robbers."

"Would robbers ring the town bell and take nothing from the man they beat nearly to death?"

My mother gasped and said nothing.

Aunt Ninya's voice waxed ominous. "No. Something terrible lurks among us. I fear for the time when it, or they, lose their paltry consciences and stop ringing bells for their victims. Poor Chen Bin lies still at Doctor Li's house, blood seeping from his ears and no mark of injury on him, but an open gash on his shin. They say he is recovering, but his head will never be right. The Council of Elders is questioning Chen Bin's friends, but I think the problem is more than our Elders can handle."

I stopped listening and walked away from the house. I walked the road south toward the village in a daze of guilt and fear. I wanted desperately to see my brothers and to know that they were all right. When I reached Sanjurra I felt an urge to slink along the shadows and behind buildings like a rat. It seemed that my neighbors were looking at me like I was some sort of demon or evil necromancer. I found Han Erh, Torin Feng and Trou Gom eating some smoked fish and roasted corn near the well on the south side of the circle. The villagers all kept a distance from them as if they were heavily poxed.

When I reached his side, Han Erh said, "Hello, Jeng. As you can see, our status has faltered some in the village." Then more quietly, he added, "They suspect us. We may be in trouble."

"I may be," I countered.

"We may be," he insisted. "None of us will ever have to stand alone again. Not while I live."

"The same from me, Jeng," Torin Feng added.

"I'm with you too, Jeng," Trou Gom said. "So are all the others."

I wanted to tell them how badly I felt for Chen Bin and for getting them into trouble, but Gener Chig was approaching us with four of the groveling fools he called his friends. Erh's jaw tightened up visibly as his nemesis approached.

Gener Chig walked right up to Erh and growled up toward his face, "Your time in this village is up, beast! A Tardor constable is on the way here to investigate your band of treasonous gangsters. What do you think of that, Erh?"

I wanted to bash his head in for talking so insolently to the best of my brothers. Han Erh was a man who never leveled such base insults at another. Only the most extreme circumstances could bring him to even utter the slightest harsh word about another person. The contrast between Erh and twisted little Gener Chig was striking. It was outrageous for Chig to talk at Erh like an angry magistrate scolding a shackled thug.

Chig waited while Erh stood seemingly impassive. Then he continued to goad the better man. "Yes, Erh. With you gone I will do whatever it takes to ruin your diseased family. I have had too much of your haughty interferences for one lifetime. Now I will win and I will have what you desire most."

Erh turned and stared blankly over Torin Feng's head. His breathing became strained and his neck taut.

I could stand no more. I struggled to keep from shouting and failed. "Go back to your daddy's store, Gener Chig!" My voice was shaking almost as badly as my hands.

Gener Chig ignored me and stepped in front of Erh, their faces close and darkening ominously. "You know what it is I will have, Erh. I will enjoy her, either willingly or by force. In fact, I hope it is by force at first. In time she will know me as a better man than you ever could be. You will live knowing that she serves my every need, and she will live knowing that you abandoned her. You've lost Erh. Why don't you just admit now that you and your bandit friends beat Chen Bin and left him to die?"

I could stand no more. I stomped my foot and shouted a few inarticulate syllables at Gener Chig. Torin Feng nearly tackled Erh in an effort to interpose himself between them. His hand shot out and pushed me firmly, but harmlessly away. Torin Feng's rear leg locked straight and his other leg bent forward as his back stiffened and his hands drew near his torso. I jumped back and blinked in disbelief at how much he looked like a praying mantis. It was more than what I saw with my eyes that revealed him so. I felt the savage and resolute presence of a giant mantis before me. I feared what might happen next and wondered why Gener Chig seemed so unafraid of the danger right there in front of him. Then I realized that he was ignorant of his peril; totally unaware of the changes taking place in the man confronting him.

Gener Chig puffed up in the face of the smaller Torin Feng. It was not often he could look down at a shorter, thinner man. "Get out of my way, you scrawny little walking stick!" he shouted.

"Back away from your betters, Chig!" Feng shouted as a crowd began to gather around us. "You have no respect for the good woman you threaten because you have no respect for any woman. And you have no respect for any woman because your mother plays the street-walker to your poxed father for nothing more than his Tardor blood-money!" A few giggles rose from the crowd, backed up by nods of agreement and a lone gasp. Gener Chig's face became a mask of shock. His fists were slowly clenching as his toadies edged away from us. Then Chig raised his fist to strike Feng and everything seemed to go into slow motion except Feng. His black robes flapped loudly for an instant as his hands flashed out toward Chig as almost invisible blurs that I could not make out. Flesh rang out with several sharp impacts before Chig fell back unconscious to the ground. His nose and right eye socket bled profusely. An instant after his head stopped bouncing in the dust, his right eyeball fell from high above and landed near him.

Torin Feng took three quick sharp steps toward Chig's toadies, who instantly fled, screaming. One of them splattered a wet trail in the dust as he ran. Someone in the quickly retreating crowd was vomiting loudly.

An old man in the crowd shouted, "Heaven help us! It's devilry in our own village!"

"Black magic and murder!" a woman shouted as she ran away.

Fearful murmurs swept through those of the crowd who were not fleeing. I suddenly felt like a prisoner on the beheading block. I knew that nobody would dare risk coming to our defenses after what had just happened. I could not expect the villagers to understand that Feng had hurt the surly young man with nothing more than his hands. I barely saw his hands with my own trained eyes.

"Burn the sorcerers!" another voice shouted from a long safe distance.

"Burn them!" several people shouted back, almost in chorus.

Feng turned toward Erh and fear slowly replaced the animal look on his face. Senya Dain came running up toward us with Onde Tor and Kor Den. The remaining villagers scrambled away from them in obvious fear. Tor carried a wooden broadsword in each hand and Den bore his long and deadly steel chain.

"What's happening?" Dain asked, glancing between Gener Chig and the three of us.

"We may have to flee," Erh answered.

"Or fight," I added.

"No," Erh said. "We can't fight our own people."

Senya Dain said, "Follow me. Tor and Den, find the others and bring them to my house. Quickly!"

Erh nodded at Tor and Den. We turned and ran out of the village after Dain.

Soon all the fighters were assembled in the front room of Senya Dain's house. There was a lot of angry discussion about what to do next, but no condemnation of our actions of the past few days. Just before sundown there came a pounding on the door. Han Erh and Senya Dain opened the door to reveal Korenda and the whole Council.

Korenda spoke with no evidence of emotion, "Judgment has been reached in the matter of your treason."

Han Erh interrupted him calmly, "Elder Korenda, please let us say a few words in our own defense."

"Judgment has already been reached, Han Erh. You may not believe it, but I argued in your favor this time. Now all arguments are finished. You have all been banished from Sanjurra and shall never again set foot within twenty miles of our village. Take what implements of magic and dark forces you have with you. Senya Dain, this farm is declared the property of the village and will be auctioned after the harvest. You all have until the rising of tomorrow's sun to take leave of your families." Then he handed a paper to Han Erh and said, "This decree bears the seal of an imperial magistrate. He would have delivered it himself, but he had business with the elder merchant Gener. Defiance of the decree automatically brings a death sentence." Then with true sorrow he said, "I'm sorry I ever sent you out into the world to become so corrupted." With that he turned and left with his Council trailing behind him.

Han Erh shut the door and remained standing with his back to us.

"What will we do?" I asked.

"Go and take leave of your parents, Jeng," he answered.

"Will we be together?" I asked him.

"Yes," Senya Dain said through clenched teeth. "Come here before sunrise and help me to take everything from this farm. Then I'm going to burn it! I wish I could poison the land!" His face was red and twitching. Tears were welling up in his eyes as he looked around at the home of his fathers and of his dead wife and children.

"Let's go," Erh said as he opened the door and walked out. "I will see you here before the sunrise."

I tried to make my visit home as short as possible. My mother cried most of the time. Father helped me to pack the travel bag I had used on my original journey to Master Kanoh.

Father put the equivalent of a man's half-year wages in the money pouch and said, "Take this, Jeng. You earned it in the fighting ring. It is a third of what I won by betting on you. Invest this in some good land with your friends. Together you can work it and prosper. If you need more in the future, just write to me."

"Write to me whether you need help or not, Jeng," Mother said as she packed food and extra clothes for me. She would not let me leave until the eastern sky brightened dangerously.

Then Father gently pried her trembling fingers from my tunic and admonished me, "Son, we know that your heart is good and that you have done no wrong. We are as proud of you as we have ever been. You must carry our family name with pride and give us many strong grandchildren."

I nodded, but could say nothing more than, "Goodbye." I raced the sun to Dain's farm. I could see angry black smoke rising into the crimson sky long before I reached the western bend of Chulin road south of Sanjurra, which led to Dain's old farm. The others were waiting for me there. They lifted several duck-filled cages as I approached. Our trunk of war art papers hung below a long wooden pole, the ends of which rested on Denju Rehn's and Amon Deng's shoulders. I caught up with the Gar Jeng at the tail end of the little caravan just as Han Erh led them out onto the road heading south.

I asked Gar Jeng, "Where does this road go besides to Chulin City."

He replied, "It passes through Ravenwood and on southward to the great river."

"I have heard weird stories about Ravenwood," I said.

"Have you also heard that we are all sorcerers?" he said. "I slept in Ravenwood on my way south to Master Denmin. It was dark and strangely quiet, but I slept there without a problem, because I didn't know where I was. Had I known it was Ravenwood, I probably would have been scared out of my head. Now that I think back on it, I don't think it's haunted at all."

"Are we going to sleep there?" I asked.

"I don't know," he replied, "but if there are evil spirits and demons there, perhaps they'll be afraid of a band of reputed sorcerers."

13 - FORMATION

We walked south on Chulin road toward Ravenwood, passing many old farms and areas of cleared land along the way. The forest thinned to patches of short spindly saplings, then gave way entirely to tall grass. We slept in the tall grass on the first night and talked, among other things, about our original journeys to find our Masters. Little was said about where we would settle. I think the rest of my friends were still in a daze over being banished from our homes. We broke camp at the rising of the sun and started south again.

As we made our way south the land began to rise and become rocky. A single grassy hill rose smooth and flat-topped off to our left. It was perhaps fifteen miles east from where the road vanished into a dark, tall forest ahead of us. The forest stretched to the east and west of the lonely hill, almost looking like a line of low dark hills itself. The sun hung low in the western sky as we approached the forest. I knew it was Ravenwood before Gar Jeng told me it was. I did not want to go in there with night coming upon us so soon. Apparently some of the others did not either; for we turned east and made for the hill. We camped at the base of the hill as the first stars appeared above. We built a large fire and I made my bed close to it. I slept fitfully, dreaming of monsters clambering out toward me from Ravenwood. In the morning, Han Erh and Tenju Gen walked up the hill to have a look around. The rest of us broke camp and prepared to resume our search for a home.

As Erh returned to us from the hill with Tenju Gen he said, "We could see Sanjurra directly to the north from up there. A fairly large lake lies behind the hill. It is hidden by Ravenwood and looks like no more than a half hour walk from the top of the hill. Shirelin Lake lies about thirty miles to the northeast of the hill. The ground up there is rocky, but fertile. We should be able to clear some good plots in time for spring planting."

We all stood silent for a while. None of us had expected to stop and set our home so soon.

Then Kanu Rahn spoke up, "I like the idea of watching over our village."

"It's no longer our village," Kavel Tom reminded him.

Senya Dain nodded in agreement to the angry sneer in Tom's voice.

Rahn countered, "Still, it would reassure me to be able to see my mother's house from my own."

Tenju Gen said, "You can't see any single houses very well, but you can see where Sanjurra is from a certain point up there. I would like to live on this hill."

"And few would dare to disturb us so close to Ravenwood," Erh said. Before anyone could object, he added, "I think we have all traveled the world enough to leave our village superstitions behind. Ravenwood is only an old dark forest. I passed through it unharmed more than a year ago. It is tangled, grim and spooky, but I never encountered anything unnatural there. I even met an old man in Sanghuei City who said he had lived there undisturbed for many years before illness drove him back to the company of other men."

Nobody responded to Erh's words until Ben Jin suggested, "Let's just camp up there for a few days before we make a firm decision. If something creepy comes up after us, we can roll Denju down the hill on it. It's perfectly defensible!"

"Hey, monkey!" Denju said with a laugh.

We started picking up our loads one by one and heading up the hill. By the time we reached the summit I was in love with the place. The thought of living on the heights reminded me of my time with Master Kanoh. On the hill I felt somehow separated from the daily concerns and nonsense of the ordinary people below; the kind of people who, through quaint superstition and ignorance, had banished me from my village, my family and my home. At the same time, I felt somehow more in touch with my family, knowing I could look down from the heights and see Sanjurra in the hazy distance.

We spent three days on the hill before every member of our party agreed to live there. We were running out of food and duck feed; so we took up a collection and seven of my brothers traveled to Bintu village on the southern shore of Shirelin Lake. They returned with two axes, four shovels, a dozen baskets of various sizes and plenty of food. Rume Lak and Ben Jin picked up the two axes and made their way down the south side of the hill into Ravenwood. They returned with ten sharp digging poles. Ten of us went to work cutting sod and removing stones from the rich dark soil. Then the others dug a forty-foot by fifteen-foot pit three feet down into the rocky dirt. We built crude, heavy, stone walls around the pit, mortared with thick grassy mud. The dragons and snakes hauled saplings from the edge of Ravenwood to beam the roof. Smaller saplings and branches provided crossbeams for the thatching. We were only rained on three times before the day that our house was finished. Another trip to Bintu village supplied both food and some lime to seal the walls of our house.

As Senya Dain, and I purchased the lime, a Bintu elder of Tardor lineage approached us. He said, "That hill you boys live on rightly belongs to the provincial governor of Gurin Province, to be tended in His Majesty's name. You people have no right to occupy it without Governor Tarkiim's favor."

With more courtesy than I thought the man deserved, Senya Dain told him, "Laws are creations of man. Ponder, if you please, that men are creations of Heaven."

The old man pursed his lips and started to speak, but stopped abruptly.

Senya Dain continued, "And so you see the rightful purpose of law. Laws are creations of man to serve man, not to subjugate him to the will of an oppressor."

The man nearly exploded with anger. "The Emperor rules because Heaven has placed the power of conquest in his hands. Whatever he does is therefore done according to the will of Heaven."

Dain countered with a smile, "Then we occupy our hill by the power Heaven has placed in us. Let us take your thought a step further. Were I to capture you now and torture you to death, I could say that whatever I did with you, I did by the will of Heaven. Further, I say that whatever any man does by force of the power within him; he does by the power and consent of Heaven. That is the furthest reach of your muddle-headed theory."

The man snorted his disagreement and walked away without another word.

Over the next fifteen months we scraped out a lean, hard living on the hill. We came to call it Ravenhill due to its proximity to the dark forest and the ravens that came to pick at our scant leavings. We bought what supplies we could afford in Bintu and raised pigs, goats, chickens, ducks and geese. Our fertile little plots yielded yams, beans, squash and other vegetables. We had not yet cleared enough ground to try raising any grains.

Since we had no distractions other than those necessary to our survival, we spent those fifteen months examining the war arts each of us had studied. We argued over what to include from each art until Senya Dain suggested voting on each fighting pattern in secret. The ballots were counted by all then burned after the result was recorded. In the end, we came up with one-hundred-forty-six fighting patterns, which we divided into six groups according to necessity and difficulty. Then we argued about how to teach the patterns to each other. Eventually we agreed to arrange each group of fighting patterns into a sort of war dance. Then we argued about the powerful merits of order as opposed to the unpredictability of chaos in our war dances. Han Erh finally ended the argument with a compromise.

He said, "How is order to be judged without chaos? And can there be true chaos without some order? The first war dance will be chaotic in honor of the unpredictable winds of fate, which brought us to Ravenhill. The second war dance will be a dance of order to reflect the order we bring from the chaos. The remaining four dances will continue that pattern, honoring each other in turn."

His solution seemed reasonable to most of us, so we readily adopted it. It took nearly two more years for us to put the dances together and work out all the problems. As the war dances progressed and each of us learned them, they became deadlier than any single art any of us had learned. Each of us saw an opportunity for his own system's strikes or blocks to be added to the other fighting patterns. Thus most of our adopted fighting patterns changed to pound an opponent much more thoroughly than any of our own. We came to accept the overkill method of fighting and began to naturally think that way. In time it came to affect everything we did. But we did not let it rule us immoderately. To do so would have lead us away from the adaptability of chaos.

I do not know how or when we began to call our system the Way of the Wind's Fist, but we all accepted it as the most fitting name. Soon thereafter we came to call our war dances Storms. We named them Tempest, Simoon, Waterspout, Whirlwind, Cyclone and Maelstrom from first to last. We agreed that, since the dragon seemed to combine all the qualities of the eight animals we used in our fighting styles, especially unpredictability, our system was an eight-animal dragon system.

Each of us studied the spear, cane, long staff, sword and double sword as we combined our diverse knowledge. Only a few of us learned the steel chain from Kor Den or the throwing of steel darts and coins from Senya Dain. Kor Den's chain and Senya Dain's darts and coins were the only steel weapons we had in our possession. Buying a sword or spear was not a possibility for men as dirt-poor as we were. So we concentrated primarily on the empty-handed forms of fighting, though most of our movements were adapted from those originally made for the sword. I learned the Storms and practiced them daily. I was able to defeat any of my compatriots when sparring. Yet I felt dishonored in that I had contributed no fighting patterns to the Storms. Master Kanoh had not taught me a single fighting pattern. So I formed my own basic fighting dance in secret. To Master Kanoh's basics I added most of those I learned in the six Storms of Wind Fist. I called my fighting dance Zephyr; the gentle breeze that comes before the storm. I practiced Zephyr every day and found that it sharpened my basic movements and made the Storms even easier for me. I knew that the others sometimes watched me practice my own fighting dance in addition to the Storms. It was not my greatest need to hide it from them. My only fear was that they might laugh at its simplicity.

One hot summer day, Erh came to me and said, "Jeng, teach us your fighting dance. The others asked me to request this of you because we all lack your powerful basics, even though we're each physically stronger than you."

"Do you really want to learn it?" I asked.

"Yes, Jeng. You can defeat any of us in a fight as you have shown many times over. So why shouldn't we want to learn what you do? We put our best fighting skills together in the six Storms; yet none of us can claim any of them as his own. Now we want to learn your fighting dance. Among the seventeen of us, only you can claim an entire dance as his own. Teach us and we will accept your instruction without question or addition."

I taught Zephyr to my brothers and they all practiced it fervently, exactly as I showed them. In time they each became much more difficult for me to defeat. I thought of old Master Kanoh on Lungshan Mountain. He had told me to believe in myself and that I knew more than I thought I did. The desire to see him and thank him grew in me each day until I could think of little else. After some weeks of discussion, I took leave of my brothers and left for Lungshan. I promised to return to them soon and refused to let any of them travel with me. I took a more direct route to Lungshan than the last time I had gone there.

I met three bandits on the way and left each of them dead on the side of the road. Each encounter surprised me with the power of my fighting art. I swore to myself that I had barely touched them with my blows; yet they reacted as if kicked by a mule. Their punches and knife slashes seemed so slow that I even wondered, at first, if they were toying with me. It was not until I destroyed the third bandit that I thought of taking his belongings for my own. They were probably ill-gotten anyway, and I figured he owed them to me for trying to hinder my path. My money purse jingled with a satisfying weight as I walked away from him. I felt like a good constable who had earned his pay by thwarting a highway robbery. The greatest part of it was that I would have had to labor long hard months for some harsh master to earn such money, while defeating the thug took only a few easy seconds.

When I reached the plateau at the top of Lungshan, I eagerly raced through the forest toward Master Kanoh's secret glade. I practiced the reverent greeting I would give to him. I happily imagined his greeting and the questions he would ask. He would surely ask if I remembered the many proverbs he had taught me. I thought of one of his favorites just as I stepped into the glade; *It is better to fight for something than to live for nothing.*

I froze after my first step into the glade. A white crane raised its head from picking among tall weeds in Master's practice circle. It called out shrill and blaring before taking gracefully to the air. The echo of its cry faded into the falling mist of the waterfall near the Master's house. Gray streaks ran down the face of the house's once clean, white walls. My own little hut was cracked and leaning with the thatch fallen in from much of the roof.

"Master Kanoh!" I called out. My voice sounded weak and uncertain after the powerful cry of the crane. I ran with leaden feet toward Master's house. The door creaked open reluctantly to my pull. A large owl fled the Master's living room through a damaged side window. I found the scant remains of Master's body in his bed. Many bottles of potions stood in attendance on the small table near him; remedies inadequate to one so old.

Kneeling beside him, I spoke the greeting I had prepared, "I greet you with joyful honor, old one." Then I bowed my head and said, "I remembered, Master Kanoh. I kept everything you taught me in my heart and I won more of a victory than any of the others. Every word you ever said to me was true and the Iron Fist was strong." Then I recited all one-hundred-forty-six fighting proverbs he had taught me.

I buried him deep beneath his practice ring that night. Into the mountain face that would serve as his headstone, I scratched; *Master Kanoh Feng, Gentle Breeze who defeated the Storms.* I gathered up the Master's precious books on medicine and war arts to take them with me. One of them caught my eye because its cover was fancier than any of the others. It was titled; 'Horse Stance, A Pristine View.' Flipping the book open, I saw the author listed as Chu Jeng of Gurin Province. Master Kanoh had transcribed my words exactly as I had written them, years ago. As I left his glade I turned and said, "You fought for excellence and mastery over yourself, old man. That is something more precious than gold."

I paid a visit to Draka Von on my way home. The warrior wept silently at the news of our Master's death. At his request, I stayed with him for three months. He refused to accept any of the Master's books, saying they were my reward for taking care of the Master's burial. We talked about the Master and the things he had taught us. Many times we practiced together and sparred. He said it was impossible for one to gain the power I had in such a short time, and that I must have been put under the magic of some powerful sorcerer. I denied that absurdity, of course, but he only gave me a strange crooked look. I traveled with him to the nearby villages and a couple of cities, where he showed me the sorry state of our people under the Tardor, warlords and thugs. I guess I had not fully noticed it before because I was young and preoccupied with other concerns. I found that Draka Von and I had much in common. He told me that our similarities came about because the Master's instruction had changed our paths of life to ones more similar. I invited him to come south and live with us on Ravenhill, but he refused, saying that he preferred the solitude of his lonely house. We parted as eternal brothers.

By the time I reached the fourth village south of Draka Von's house, the news had spread that a skinny young man was traveling south with a load of precious books and gold. Before I traveled halfway home, the story had changed to say that a great sorcerer warlord was traveling south with demon guardians at his command. I had to hire two porters to help carry the booty I collected from the various thugs who had tried to bar my way.

Kavel Tom and Denju Rehn were the first to spot me as I approached Ravenhill. They ran down to me and Denju immediately lifted me over his head and spun me around.

He shouted, "You slow-witted little prankster. Why did you stay away for so long? We were all worried! Han Erh was getting ready to send a group of us out to find you."

Kavel Tom looked at the valuable broadsword dangling at my side and at the bundles carried by my porters and asked, "Where did you get all these goods?"

"I bought most of it," I said as Denju set me down. "Some of it was given to me directly by robbers who died for their cause or gave it to me in exchange for their lives. I have gifts for all my brothers."

Then Tom asked, "What is wrong, Jeng? You look different. You look older in an unpleasant way, as if something was taken from you."

I answered him in the only way I could. "I've seen too much death of the wrong kind and not enough of the right kind. I've watched our countrymen wither under the burden of oppression. I suppose my youth was taken from me in addition to most everything else I've ever cared for."

I paid my porters and dismissed them.

105

Denju summoned a bit of contrived cheer and said, "What do you think of these robes? We all have them now."

I walked around him, examining his robes. They were excellent looking; black with a forest-green trim. A rich-looking mantle and hood topped the robes and made the big man look rather monkish. The back of the mantle bore a broken green circle separated by an open cross. I stopped in front of him and said, "Good for stalking through a dark forest, I suppose, but they look a bit foreign."

"Not for stalking or fighting," Denju said. "We have fighting clothes, too. These are only for ceremonies and festivals."

"Ceremonies?" I asked.

"Yes, Jeng," Tom answered. "A great many things have happened since you left. Good things. A man came to Ravenhill from the west, far beyond the empire. He only asked for a place to stay for the night, but after we heard his words, we begged him to stay for several weeks."

I stared at him for a moment. His eyes shone with a joyful light that I had never seen before.

I said, "I brought swords for each of us."

"That is what his Master said!" Denju exclaimed. "He said, 'Do not suppose it is peace I bring to the world. It is not peace I have come to bring, but a sword.' He came to bring peace to each individual heart!"

"Is that all he said?"

Tom laughed and said, "He brought all the best teachings of our revered philosopher, Kung Fu Tsu, to life, and those of the Enlightened one and old Lao Tan as well. His teachings made everything fit together and make sense."

I looked back at my porters walking off in the distance and, for an instant, felt like following them. I turned back to my compatriots and said, "Let's get these things up to the hill."

14 - DRAGONS

As we trudged up the hill, I saw that our lonely long-house was no longer alone. Several smaller houses stood along side it and a tower was under construction. I met Han Erh at the top of the hill and he smiled down at me. When I reached him, he glanced at the sword at my side and said, "I was worried about you, Jeng. Are you well?"

I watched Denju and Tom walk toward the long-house with my bundles and said, "I'm fit, Erh. How is it with you and the rest of them?"

"We're all blessed with happiness, health and peace," he said. "Ravenhill has become a splendid place to live."

"Ravenhill may be comfortable for us, Erh, but the rest of the empire is a nightmare for our people."

Erh looked directly in my eyes and said, "Chu Jeng, when right paths of nature call you to violence of action, that violence need not take your peace of soul. We hunt this region for bandits without letting the hunt destroy our happiness and harmony." He saw the look on my face and said, "I'm glad you're home, little Brother."

"What has the stranger from the west done to you? Is everybody here a philosopher now?"

Erh laughed and said, "He answered every question we had and raised ten-thousand more. In one sense every man is a philosopher. Some are just better at it than others. That is the choice, Jeng; either be good at it or poor at it, the same as with our way of fighting. Either strive for wisdom or be a contented fool. Your eyes are open now, and you see the pain of our people. That unpleasant vision begins the natural pain of wisdom. Now open your heart and receive the peace of Heaven."

I wanted peace, but did not believe in it. I could not believe it was right for me to have peace when there was so much oppression and injustice heaped upon my people. I resisted what seemed like mindless blissful talk of my fellow warriors for about a week. Then one night I stood looking down on the evening torches of Sanjurra far in the moonless distance. My guts were wrenching with the pain of my own weakness in the face of the empire's injustice. There in the flickering fires of Sanjurra were my parents living within my sight and I could not even go to them. I looked up at the stars and felt so weak and insignificant. I walked to the long-house where my brothers were saying their evening prayers. Pushing the door open, I walked inside.

"If this man-God of yours cared so much as to die for me, then I am ready to turn my life over to Him. Let me see if He can do anything with it." I walked through my kneeling brothers and knelt before their symbol of the tortured Son of God. Han Erh and several others laid their hands on my shoulders and head. They prayed quietly as I did. Suddenly I felt something like heavenly rain pouring down through me and washing away the blackness of my embittered heart. I laughed and cried at the same time and wanted to dance. My brothers rejoiced with me and we were one. We were truly one in a way that I could never explain to anyone who has not experienced that heavenly cleansing.

The years that followed were full of divine energy and bliss for me. We finished building the tower and supplemented our agricultural income with booty from slain or subdued bandits. It took some talking on my part to convince my brothers to confiscate the possessions of the bandits we defeated. I finally persuaded them by saying we could give some of the money to widows and those who cared for orphans. We ended up giving the majority of it to the poor. Whenever we hunted, I fought without anger and always tried to allow my enemies a chance to yield their weapons in exchange for their lives. We had to hunt farther and farther for thugs each time we went out. We watched the villages of our region prosper without the constant strain of rampant crime. Then the Tardor tax collectors and the local warlords' tax collectors hit the people even harder. Somehow it did not frustrate me as it would have before I returned from Lungshan to be reborn on Ravenhill. My brothers and I simply continued doing what we knew was right and sought for a better solution to the problem.

All but a few of the villagers in the area shied away from us whenever we came to town. At first I thought it was because we had all taken to wearing swords or other weapons at our sides. The widows and orphans flocked to us, of course, but the others often indulged in odd rumors or the more familiar and more irritating rumors about black magic. One spring day I walked into the market square of Bintu village with Erh and Denju.

A little boy saw us coming from a distance, pointed toward us and shouted, "The dragons are coming this way!" as he ran out of the opposite side of the square.

We stopped and looked at each other since there was no one else around us. We went about our business and then heard a woman mention the name dragons in reference to us. I turned to look at her and she quickly walked away.

Denju asked the old merchant who was selling us a few sacks of powdered lime, "Why did that lady and the little boy call us dragons?"

"Don't mind them," the old man replied. "People just get scared about things they don't know. They call you the Seventeen Dragons of Wulin because you protect us and live at the south of the five lake region and right on the border of the haunted forest. But, you have always been good customers with me and treated me fair good. I was never one to be calling you men dragons like the rest of them." He jerked his thumb toward the milling crowd at the other side of the square. "They are also calling you 'God worshipers' and say that's another curse for the empire."

I smiled and said, "Perhaps it's a curse to the Tardor tyrants who seek to rule men's hearts and minds, casting them into despair. Then perhaps the light of truth seems a curse to those who fear stepping out of the darkness of paganism and ancestor worship. But then, my countrymen consider the Tardor invaders to be the greatest of curses."

The old man nodded and said, "There are too many of them Tardor moving into our village. The way they treat us, I think they consider us a curse, except when we're slaving for them."

Han Erh said, "Tyranny is the worst of curses, whatever its source. Whether the cause is banditry, ignorance, wine, greed, sloth or oppressive government; whether men are oppressed by others or by their own vices; that which lowers a man's nature to ugliness and shame is a curse beyond death."

The man grunted and said, "Most of our people were oppressed by our own nobles before the Tardor came. The Tardor are only the last of a long line of oppressors. The sick thing is how they say we 'barbaric' people are too ungrateful for all they have done to 'civilize' us. They ought to be stomped!" Then he suddenly lowered his head, looked around with just his eyes and would say no more.

After we made our purchase and walked away with three bags of lime, Erh smiled at me and said, "They call us dragons? I like that!"

We called ourselves Dragons from that day on and began calling each other by Dragon names such as Forest Mist, Fire Wind, Jade Eye, Spear Tail, Shadow Wing and Golden Claw. Our way of knowledge increased and unified into a solid, logical system of power and the perfecting of our beings. Our world expanded before our eyes and revealed itself to us in the astounding glory of creation. We developed the Eight Aspect Path of perfection. In time we learned to control the states of our beings, and that turned out to be even more powerful than our fighting system. For us, working, fighting, speaking and thinking all merged into one unified way of power. It came to be that some of us could often confront a highway robber and use our Dragon speech to talk him into turning himself into the local constable without him even knowing what he was doing. We would have him give us all his weapons and money first, of course.

The rumors of our using black magic grew with the increase in our natural powers of self control. The rumors were all nonsense of course. People called whatever they did not understand, magic, as the merchant of Bintu had said. And they understood little of what we did as Dragons. The earthly tongue of our people did not serve to speak of the mysteries we had discovered in our studies, so we developed terms that suited our purposes. The sounds of these secret terms we borrowed mostly from the language of a trader we came to know from the Bunjeeb region of the Southern Kingdom. The terms blossomed in number, relationship and complexity to become Keloram; the tongue of the Dragons. We became further and further removed from the world in our philosophies and our way of life. In time we came to referring to all other people as outsiders, knowing that they could not possibly understand our ways.

One night I came upon an amazing truth as I gazed long at the stars from the roof of our tower. I used to climb up there to recline and ponder the heavens. I thought it strange that as I progressed on the Dragons' Path the world became more disgusting to me and yet I gained more inner peace. The blind vanity of mankind's affairs wearied me and yet I was strengthened by knowledge of the vanity. It was a paradox of opposing truths, like the fact that the way of nature is harmony through conflict. I wondered at how much I had changed and then thought that I was the same person that I was as a child and yet a completely different person; different in mind, body and every other aspect of my being. It came to me then that true wisdom is an ability to accept the paradoxical nature of the deepest truths.

One warm summer night, Senya Dain and Tenju Gen returned from hunting in the forbidden area around Sanjurra. They knocked on the door to the tower's upper room where Erh and I were meditating.

"Come in," Erh said, blinking away the effects of his long meditation.

Tenju Gen, whom we called Forest Mist, said "Something bad happened last night."

Erh waited for further explanation then asked, "You didn't get yourselves recognized in the forbidden area, did you?"

Senya Dain exclaimed, "No! It's nothing like that. It's... much worse, actually."

I was growing impatient with their lack of clarity. "What did you do?" I asked.

"We beheaded two of Warlord Kang's tax collectors," Tenju Gen blurted out.

Senya Dain added even worse news, "Then we sent their heads back to their master with the third tax collector."

Tenju Gen continued by saying, "We told him that Sanjurra village belonged to the Dragons of Wulin and that Kang's men had better never return. We tried to terrify him as much as possible, Erh. Maybe the message will frighten Kang into staying away."

"Well," Erh said thoughtfully, "you have definitely terrified me. What would possibly motivate you to do such a foolhardy thing? Seventeen men can't fight a warlord's army."

Tenju Gen said, "They were dragging Han Jenya into the forest to rape her."

Erh jumped to his feet with his hands in tiger claw form, then composed himself. He walked to the window and leaned on the sill, gazing toward Sanjurra. "Have we been gone so long? My cousin was..." He struggled to control his anger. "Jenya was only a baby when I left home!"

"She is eleven years old now, Erh," Tenju Gen told him.

Without turning from the window, Erh asked the Dragons, "Does she know who you are?"

"No," Tenju Gen answered. "She only knows we are Dragons. And she knows what we did."

Erh winced and said, "You didn't make her watch that, did you?"

"No, sir," Tenju Gen said, "but we explained it to try to comfort her and assure her that she would never be attacked like that again."

I said, "The people of Sanjurra must be terrified! We can't leave them to be slaughtered, Erh."

"There are only seventeen of us," he said.

111

I stood up and said, "It is better to fight for something than to live for nothing, even if we die."

Erh turned toward us and the other two Dragons nodded their agreement with me. He stared at us for some time then said, "Call all the others to council in the long-house."

The three of us left to brief the others and bring them together.

Once assembled, we sat on the stone floor around the small fire pit near the south end of the long-house. Anger shone from many faces in the flickering firelight. Fear shone from a few others. The rest seemed impassive as we waited for Han Erh to enter.

Amon Deng sat glaring at Senya Dain and Tenju Gen. His lips were pressed to a thin line under his dark glaring eyes and his breathing came fast.

Dain raised his hands palm up and calmly asked, "Amon Deng, are you the sort of Dragon who would let three strong men rape an innocent child of your own village?"

Deng shouted back, "We will have no village when Kang's troops behead everyone in Sanjurra and burn it to the ground!"

"Then would you have left her to them?" Gen said with what sounded like a taunting patience.

"I would have killed them and buried their bodies in the forest; not slapped the most ruthless and powerful warlord of our region in the face."

Dain's voice raised and crackled. "We have all been lazily and cowardly plucking single leaves from an ugly weed that begs to be ripped out by the roots! Ripped out by the filthy roots and burned! You could play the hero and save that little girl while allowing scores of others to be raped, enslaved and murdered in the vicinity of Ravenhill! I can't live that way any longer. I won't! Something has to be done about it. We can't be everywhere, so our reputation must be everywhere."

Gis Erh jumped to his feet next to Amon Deng and shouted, "We are not an army!"

A babble of angry and concerned voices erupted in various arguments.

"The number of attackers is not so important as the number of attacks," I shouted above the din.

The arguing stopped immediately and every head turned my way. Amon Deng growled, "What under Heaven is that supposed to mean?"

I stood up and said, "I mean that we need only control the number of attacks that Kang's army can send against us at one time. My Master said that a warrior needs only three things to defeat a thousand men. He needs to be better than each of them individually, control the number of attacks he has to deal with at any one time and have the endurance to fight fiercely until the end."

Gis Erh said, "Kang's is a trained army, Jeng. It's not going to form seventeen lines to take fair turns with us."

General laughter broke out, mixed with scornful, angry comments.

Then Han Erh stepped from the shadows of the north end of the long-house and walked to my side. The noise subsided right away.

He sat down and those of us who were standing sat down after him. He said, in his usual calm manner, "Jeng's way is to control the number of attacks, the way of my Master is to choose the time and conditions of battle. Gar Jeng's way of the Coiling Serpent is to not be seen until he attacks. Amon Deng's way is to attack with unbridled ferocity to crush his opponent in spirit and then body. Tenju Gen's way is to disappear and be impervious to attack. Rume Lak's way is to strike the enemy when he is down, so that he may never rise to attack him again. We should, therefore, be able to come up with a deadly strategy together." He stared at each of us for a moment and said, "Kang's arrow is already loosed and whistles toward us. Let he who thinks it a good defense to attack his own brother do it now."

Torin Feng stood up and complained to Erh, "You failed to mention that my way is to strike with the lightning-fast attack that leaves the enemy no chance to react."

"That's right," Ben Jin said, jumping to his feet and laughing. "And my way is to deceive the enemy into wasting his resources on a frontal defense while I flank him!"

General laughter broke out again, but it was the laughter of relief. I must not have been the only one who was glad to have Erh's stabilizing leadership among us.

Ben Jin straightened his robes and sat down with exaggerated dignity, saying, "All Right then. That's the kind of respect I was looking for."

We all laughed even harder at the monkey stylist.

When we settled down, Han Erh said, "Tenju Gen, I think the proper time has come for you to reveal your secret weapon to the other Dragons. It may be just the thing to rally their confidence and unity of will. The rest of them need to see it before we can work it into our plans for dealing with Kang's army."

Tenju Gen disappeared for a while as the rest of us reconvened outside.

When Gen reappeared, he stood off in the distance with a small torch in his hand, and said, "Amon Deng, take a stick from the woodpile and throw it at me. Throw it hard!"

While Deng walked over to the wood pile, I saw Tenju Gen take a drink from a small black waterskin. Deng walked back to the rest of us with a stick as long and thick as a man's leg. He grunted as he slung the stick as hard as he could at the waiting Dragon. Tenju Gen quickly brought the small torch up to his face and seemed to look through the flames at the heavy missile that whirled its way toward his head. I thought he had better move quickly or our number would soon be reduced to sixteen. At the last instant, a bright cone of flame roared from the Dragon's mouth and engulfed the stick. Gen leaped to the side, drew his sword and slashed the flaming stick as it sped past him. The waterskin swung to his side on a lanyard as the flaming stick whirled into the darkness.

The Dragons burst into wild exultant cheers as Gen raised his sword and stared at it.

When the cheers subsided, Erh said, "Blowing a mouthful of oil through a flame is only one way our brother has shown me how to throw fire on an enemy."

Chen Ner raised his voice, "But, why did he keep it secret from us?"

Erh shrugged and said, "That's the way of our brother, the Forest Mist. I believe he has also kept many secrets from me. I do not begrudge him his way, though. If he or his Masters developed such deadly secrets, then we will have to do the same and invent our own additional ways of power."

Once back inside the long-house, we discussed the many possibilities of using fire against our more powerful enemies. I listened to my brothers freely and creatively make battle plans using the special talents of each Dragon. Erh interjected his own thoughts only when necessary to bring them back on track. His perfect face looked both intense and serene as he oversaw our efforts. I could not keep my eyes from being drawn back to him again and again. He was our true leader and we all loved him for the life and unity he gave to us. I wanted to be like him. Somehow I knew that one day I would be like him in leadership, but would never equal him in his natural personal excellence.

We knew that Warlord Kang's tax collector would take a week to return to him. Erh figured it would take another week to outfit, supply and assemble his army. Then the army would take about a week and a half to travel to Sanjurra. Therefore, we safely had about two weeks to practice our battle strategies before engaging the enemy. We discussed our plans for about three days. The weeks that followed were the most intense period of training of my life except for the time I spent with Master Kanoh Feng on Lungshan. We altered and refined our plans as we practiced implementing them. Tenju Gen carefully taught Han Erh, Senya Dain and Trou Gom the ways of projecting fire. Kavel Tom hired a man from Bintu village to ride a fast horse all the way to Jangtoh City and back. He returned to the base of Ravenhill with a package of deadly poisons. Erh rewarded him generously in addition to Tom's payment. When the time was right, we set out to intercept the enemy on Gwenje road north of Sanjurra. We hauled as much supplies and weapons as we could safely carry in silence. I marveled at the warrior's resolve that shone from the faces of my compatriots. There was an intensity of life in them that I had never seen before. I felt it in myself too. Somehow being close to death made life more real and precious to me. It was the richest time of my life.

15 - BATTLE

We spied Warlord Kang's vanguard about seventy miles north of Sanjurra on Gwenje road. As night had not yet fallen, Erh ordered us to fall back into the shadows of the forest. We were all dressed in black battle clothes with foliage tied onto our arms, heads and legs. Our faces had not yet been painted, so we crouched down and covered all but our eyes with our gloved hands. I counted four wagons, and about one-hundred-fifty troops, some of whom I guessed were sergeants by their armor and swaggering manner. A big man in splendid armor rode a spirited black warhorse in front of the troops. Behind him rode five strong-looking officers on warhorses. We followed their slow, noisy march south toward our families as the sky darkened. Eventually they turned east into the forest near the ruined foundations of a long-gone farmhouse.

"Leave six men here to set up a toll." I heard the commander say to one of his officers.

The officer turned his horse immediately, rode to the back and barked a few commands to one of the sergeants. The sergeant and six of his men began setting up the simple toll-station immediately. By tradition all traffic along Gwenje road would be shut down except for those who paid the commander's heavy toll. Imperial troops, officials and those with seals of imperial favor would be exempt, of course. The commander apparently intended to encamp his forces for the night. One of the officers set a group of about twenty men to fan out and scout the area for trouble. The scouts tramped careless and grumbling through the forest. Han Erh quickly ordered us to retreat from the area until the enemy settled in for the night.

We secured a position in a thicket-lined hollow southeast of the old farm clearing. We gathered close and Erh sent the Dragons to patrol nearby for short turns in pairs.

"I counted only about one-hundred-sixty men," Han Erh whispered. "Kang's army is supposed to number nearly a thousand men."

I whispered back, "Perhaps he figures he won't need more than this to raze the village and punish those who killed his tax collectors."

Erh said, "We will wait for the third hour of full darkness and rest here in the meantime. Those who can sleep should do so. Then Tenju Gen will lead Cheng Ner, Trou Gom and Gar Jeng to check on how the enemy is arrayed for the night. You four are the best at slinking around unseen in the dark. Remember to paint your faces before you go."

117

The hours passed quickly and I hardly slept at all. Erh woke Tenju Gen up and the four spies completely painted their faces in green with black tiger stripes. They crept off into the night with a prayer from Erh. They returned about two hours later. I had not even tried to sleep during their absence. I was set for the battle and wanted to get to it.

We gathered around while Tenju Gen quietly made his report to Erh. We all listened carefully. The Forest Mist diagrammed his report by scratching a map into the dirt as he spoke. "There are no enemy patrols at all," he said. "They have the six men and one sergeant at their toll-station on Gwenje road. In the glade they built small watch fires at the northeast, northwest, southwest and southeast edges of the forest. The southern watch fires have only one sentry each; the northern have two each. The sentries are not very vigilant and watch mostly inward at their own people. Between the two northern watch fires sleep forty troops with four sergeants. Between the two western watch fires sleep another forty troops with four sergeants. Between the two southern watch fires five small tents are set with, we assume, one officer sleeping in each. A vigilant sentry stands facing south from the officer's tents. He looks around constantly. Just south of the northeast watch fire, another twenty troops sleep with their two sergeants. Another fourteen sleep with one sergeant just north of the officer's tents. Four supply wagons, a supply area and the weapons cache lie in the center of the glade. Twenty more troops and two sergeants sleep just south of the supply and weapons area. Twenty-two horses are tied up to a long chain around the south of the wagons. To the north of the supply area a large ornate tent stands with two large guards and a sergeant. The commander's black horse is tethered just north of the tent. That is the entire layout. None of the sleeping troops appear to be armed with more than the personal weapons they might own in addition to their issued weapons. The sergeants however have swords lying next to them and a spear thrust into the ground near them. If you please, sir, The time to strike is now."

My stomach knotting with urgency as Erh discussed the situation and made battle plans with Tenju Gen. The rest of us painted our faces and looked truly frightening, I thought, in our battle gear. Kor Den sat contemplating his deadly steel chain while the others fingered their swords or quietly stretched their muscles. Senya Dain stood in a battle stance and practiced finding the scores of eleven-inch steel spikes and poisoned coins

118

he had set in specially made holsters on his thighs and arms. His eyes were filled with a terrifying lust for battle. At last, my mind settled on an image of Master Kanoh's face. Somehow I saw him smiling peacefully and looking into my eyes as an accomplished friend rather than scowling at me as a bumbling student. I looked upon that image in my mind until Erh called us together.

Erh smiled and said, "This is the plan, Brothers. I will lead Tenju Gen, Gar Jeng, and Senya Dain from the south to silently kill the southern sentry at the officer's tents. Trou Gom will simultaneously kill the southeastern watch fire sentry and Cheng Ner will kill the southwestern sentry. If possible, all sentries and sleeping troops will be killed with poisoned daggers to prevent them from calling out. Kavel Tom will provide the poison before we set out. Don't nick yourselves with the poisoned blades! Tenju Gen and Gar Jeng will sneak north to the commander's tent, using the supplies and wagons for concealment, while Senya Dain and I kill the sleeping officers. Amon Deng and Kavel Tom will watch the northeastern sentries until they see Tenju Gen and Gar Jeng strike the guards at the commander's tent. They will silently slay the sentries at the same time as the commander's guards are slain. Denju Rehn and Rume Lak will watch the northwestern sentries and do the same. Tenju Gen will immediately enter the commander's tent and kill him before he wakes up. That should take care of all the sentries and the officers. Senya Dain and I will guard the weapons cache with Tenju Gen's breath of fire. Chu Jeng and Ben Jin will wait for the first sounds of battle and then slay the six troops and sergeant at the toll station. They will then rush to join us in the glade. Gis Erh and Onde Tor will rush the waking troops from the west. Kor Den and Torin Feng will likewise rush in on them from the east and Kanu Rahn will enter from the southwest and team up with Cheng Ner. Those who have slain the sentries will join us in attacking the regular troops. We must throw the enemy into complete panic and confusion, so try to kill the sergeants first. Silently kill as many sleeping men as you can before the others wake up. At the instant that silence is no longer an option, Torin Feng, Trou Gom, Kanu Rahn, Gis Erh, Denju Rehn and Amon Deng will remove the sealed lids of these buckets of flammable oil and douse the masses of enemy troops before they rise from their bedding. Their partners will then throw a torch on the doused men to light the oil. Leave only a handful of the enemy alive and then disappear into the forest to the east on my command. Speak only the language of the Dragons when in battle."

He repeated the battle plan twice again and everyone said they knew their duties. Then he made sure we all knew each other's duties. After that, he covered several alternate plans and contingencies, warning us that no plan for battle survives initial contact. When certain we were ready, Erh led us in prayer then led us to battle. Not a word was spoken as we crept toward the glade with our gear in hand. Ben Jin and I sneaked up to where we could see the two swordsmen on the road at the toll station. Their sergeant and four additional armed men slept just off the road behind a thick cluster of trees. We waited an interminable time for the battle to begin. My legs cramped and I thought I would sweat the war paint off my face. I was reassured by the fact that sweat was running down Ben Jin's face and leaving his oily paint intact.

Suddenly I heard a scream of terror through the trees behind me. That was our signal. We looked wide eyed at each other for an instant and then burst forward to the attack. Several angry or confused shouts followed the scream in the glade. The swordsmen on the road reached the edge of the road just as we burst through the trees. Their faces contorted in shock as if they did not know what we were. Or perhaps, they had mistakenly thought the trouble was only in the glade where the shouts were occurring. I swept the head from my opponent with my broadsword as Ben Jin hacked the sword-arm and one leg from the other. We spun on our heels and rushed instantly back at the four wakening troops and their sergeant. I slashed the bellies of two of them as Ben Jin engaged the other two in sword play. The sergeant was awake and shouting with a spear in his hands. He instantly brought the spear haft down toward my head. I jumped to the side and brought my sword down upon the spear, pinning it to the ground for an instant. Just then, I heard the roar of flames, instantly followed by the terrorized and agonized screams of scores of men. A wave of confusion and fear swept over the sergeant's face and he glanced toward the terrible noise. I stomped his spear in half and chopped off his head before he had a chance to look back. Ben Jin had already killed one of his opponents and I leaped forward to slash the legs from under the second. Jin then brought his broadsword down and ended the man's pain.

We rushed toward the glade without a word, killing three half-naked, unarmed troops who fled blindly from the Dragons. As we entered the glade, the smell of blood and burned flesh and hair struck my nose like a flying rock. A sergeant rushed at Han Erh with a spear leveled at his belly. A long cone of flame shot from Erh's mouth and engulfed the sergeant, turning him into a running, screaming, flailing whirlwind of fire. Kang's troops were shouting in fear and utter confusion. They called for their commander, officers and sergeants, most of whom already lay forever silent. Some of the troops who had weapons fought their way toward the weapons cache and died at the hands of Erh and Dain.

Ben Jin and I fought our way into the glade, though most of the fighting was over. More of Kang's troops carried inferior personal weapons than Tenju Gen and his spies had predicted. In the distance, I watched one swordsman bolt for the horses. Kor Den's chain wrapped around the man's neck and jerked him off his feet. Den whipped the chain overhead in two vertical arcs that slammed brutally down on the writhing man, who then stopped moving. Even from across the glade and through the din of battle I heard Den's chain whistle through the air and crunch the warrior's bones.

A soldier rushed toward me with the broken remains of a sergeant's spear. He threw the rear half of the spear shaft at my legs and immediately thrust the point at my throat. The shaft bounced off my shins just before I deflected the spear point with my broadsword. I kicked the charging man in the ribs and felt them snap. As he stumbled past me, I slashed through his kidneys and lower spine. Two of his compatriots rushed me from my left side. Ben Jin hacked the sword arm from the first, and the second stumbled clumsily toward me to fall writhing on the ground with one of Senya Dain's poisoned coins imbedded in the side of his neck. I could hear Amon Deng growling and roaring like a tiger as he hacked his way through the enemy. Trou Gom was spitting fire and swaying gracefully as he made his way through the remaining enemy to the south. Fires were everywhere, most of them inanimate, while others were loud and running aimlessly or flopping around on the ground.

Soon no more than ten of Kang's troops remained alive, bewildered and terrified in the glade. None remained where Ben Jin, Gis Erh, Onde Tor and I had gathered. I was panting hard and my black battle clothes were heavy with blood. The others looked the same. Ben Jin's eyes had a crazed look that reflected the angry fires around us. The glade seemed to have instantly grown quiet except for the crackle of flames, panting

Dragons and a few blubbering soldiers.

"Come, now!" Han Erh shouted in our secret language.

We all disappeared into the forest as quickly as the battle had started. Once the first shout had been raised, the remarkable battle took no longer than it would take for a man to walk from one side of Sanjurra's market circle to the other. The Dragons gathered in the forest and checked each other for wounds. My shins were lumped, but I was otherwise unharmed. A few of the others had taken minor cuts and thumps. Senya Dain had taken a spear in the back of his leg when twelve armed men had rushed him at once. He and Han Erh killed them all quickly without the use of fire, but one of them had wounded the Green Dragon stylist just before falling.

"You will die without a doctor's help and the nearest doctor is in Sanjurra," Han Erh told Senya Dain.

Tenju Gen spoke up immediately, "I will take him there."

"No," Senya Dain protested. "I'll not have you earn a death sentence for my sake. I can make it if you just keep some pressure on the wound until the bleeding stops."

"The bleeding is not going to stop without Doctor Li's help," Erh said. "I will take you there."

"I will!" Trou Gom said.

"So will I!" Gis Erh shouted.

"I will go with them," Denju Rehn said. "I fear no imperial death warrant."

"I will too," Kor Den said.

"Let me take him!" Amon Deng growled, his voice still hoarse and filled with blood lust from the battle.

Each one of us, in turn, promised to go with Senya Dain to Sanjurra. We returned to the deserted glade and loaded the four wagons up with the weapons, supplies and other booty. We hitched the work horses to the wagons and six of us mounted the warhorses while Han Erh knelt on one of the wagons with his hands pressed down on Senya Dain's wound. I struggled for control over my headstrong warhorse the whole way to Sanjurra and was exhausted almost beyond my strength by the time we arrived. Keeping my left hand wrapped in the reigns was the only way I could keep control of him each time he threw me to the ground. We reached Sanjurra just before sunrise and rode into the market circle to ring the town bell.

Those villagers who came out, huddled in fear at the north end of the circle and would not talk to us. We must have looked terrible in our painted faces and blood-soaked battle clothes. The stomping, snorting warhorses and military supply wagons probably did not soften our images much either.

At last, Elder Korenda approached us and said, "What do you want with our village, warriors? We are at your service."

I realized then that he didn't recognize us.

Han Erh answered him with, "We have destroyed Warlord Kang's army before it reached this village to annihilate you. We bring you his commander's head in exchange for Doctor Li's help for our fallen Brother."

"Only this few of you remain?" Korenda asked with a touch of honest sympathy in his voice.

"We are all who attacked them" Han Erh said. "Only our brother in this wagon is injured."

Elder Korenda took a few quick steps forward and stared wide eyed at Han Erh. "You are..."

Han Erh shouted, "We're the Seventeen Dragons of Wulin. Sanjurra belongs to us now." Then he leaned toward Korenda, glared with fire in his eyes and growled, "There are no other names for us that any man who wishes to live will ever say aloud!" Korenda fell to his knees and pressed his forehead to the dirt. "Call Doctor Li to us, now," Erh commanded the Elder, who jumped to his feet and ran for the doctor's house. He motioned a few gawking villagers away as he ran and they fled with him.

The Doctor came to the wagon and bound the flesh of Senya Dain's leg together with fine threads of boiled wildcat intestine and a curved needle. Senya grunted and moaned very quietly the whole time, but did not flinch or flex against the doctor's efforts. The Doctor apologized to the Dragon and often winced as he worked, sucking air through his clenched teeth in empathy for Dain's suffering. He worked on Dain for nearly four hours. By the time he finished the Dragon was too weak to talk. The doctor gave potions and instructions to Han Erh for Senya Dain's continued care.

Before Doctor Li left the wagon, he leaned forward and whispered to Senya Dain, "My bets were all on you so many years ago. I hope you gained vengeance on those who took your family." He smiled and gently patted the weak Dragon's shoulder.

Senya Dain closed his eyes and, despite his bloody clothes and war paint, looked as peaceful as I have ever seen him.

As the doctor had worked on Dain's wound, the rest of us prayed while Kor Den, Amon Deng and Gis Erh cataloged our booty. They made a list for Han Erh. We had collected from Kang's defeated army;

190 swords
22 recurve bows
361 arrows
31 spears
enough armor to fully equip about twenty-five men
6 trained warhorses
16 work horses
4 military type supply wagons
6 bags of copper and silver coin
6 large bags of rice
3 large bags of beans
7 large bags of yams
4 large bags of oats
3 large jars of oil
8 water barrels
miscellaneous supplies such as cooking pots, ropes, chains, tent materials, etc.

Han Erh told us to leave one bag of coin, two wagons, eight of the work horses, one bag each of rice, beans, yams and oats for the villagers. "Here is some of what Kang has stolen from you over the years," Han Erh said to Korenda as we prepared to leave.

We marched east out of the village and turned south at the crossroads. We traveled south for less than a mile when a large group of villagers emerged from the forest and blocked our path. They advanced on us and we recognized them as our own families. As soon as I saw my mother's eyes the others all faded from my vision. I kicked my horse to a trot and rode to her side. It was only when I dismounted that I saw how short she was. I had forgotten that eleven years had passed. Mother used to tower over me, I remembered, as she held me tight and pressed her head against my chest.

She began wiping the war paint from my face and I noticed that her hair was streaked with gray. "Let me see you, Jeng. Heaven's gain, but you're a man!" she exclaimed. "It has been so long that I thought maybe you…" She stopped and bit her lip.

"I think of you every day, Mother. I watch the torches of Sanjurra every night from our hill and pray for you and Father." Then I looked around and said, "Where is Father?"

She said, "He is gone on from us, Jeng. A fever took many of our village three years ago. Now I live with my sister, Jenya, and her family."

"Our farm?" was all I could say.

"I sold it, Jeng. I have more than enough to live on for the remainder of my years."

Suddenly I understood Senya Dain's painful remarks of eleven years before when he lost the land of his fathers.

I heard Han Erh calling us to leave for home. I knew he wanted to get Senya Dain to rest and proper care on Ravenhill before nightfall. Only with the horses and wagons did we have a chance to get him home as soon as should be, and only if we hurried.

"Goodbye, Mother," I said, hugging her tight and suddenly realized that I had never written her as I had promised. "I will write to you this time," I said as I mounted my rebellious warhorse. I could hear the others taking leave of their relatives and climbing into the wagons or mounting their horses. I rode up beside the wagon that carried Han Erh and Senya Dain.

To Erh I said, "May I keep this horse?"

"Keep him," he replied, laughing at my continual struggle with the spirited animal. "He obviously likes you. I can see he wants to stay with you."

"Yes," I replied. "He cares enough to work me like Master Kanoh used to. I think I'll call him Lungshan."

16 - GUARDIANS

For the first six months, the horses were more trouble than they were worth. The warhorses were all rebellious stallions and had to be kept apart, except when mounted. Hauling water and food for them was a full-time occupation until we hired a hostler, named Renje, from Bintu and built a corral and stables at the edge of our hidden lake. The hostler refused to stay at the stables alone in Ravenwood. So, for a few months we took turns staying with him for a few days at a time, which proved to be an invaluable education in the care of horses. We hired more help from Bintu and built a narrow fenced road from the lake to a very large fenced pasture at the base of our hill. The mares and geldings had free reign between the stables, lake and pasture. The stallions were still difficult, but the hostler did most of the work with them.

Though he had learned some art of warrior horsemanship from his time studying in the south, Han Erh decided we needed more training in that art. So he traveled for two months to the Sanjao wild region in the far northwest of the empire. There he hired an old horse warrior from the nomadic Manjugom tribes to train us in horsemanship. The grizzled and scarred old man barely understood our language, but he understood the horses and they understood him. His name was Subai Tahn and he claimed his proud ancestry from the great warlord Tahns of the Manjugwe Dynasty. He respected the Dragons because our reputation had spread almost to the Sanjao wild region and he heard rumor of us as soon as he and Han Erh had entered the more civilized parts of the empire. For some unknown reason, Subai Tahn wasted no time in deciding that he was Renje's master. The old horseman lorded it over the simple hostler and often resorted to beatings when the language barrier proved too frustrating. Subai Tahn was always patient and respectful with the Dragons, though. We learned to fight from horseback almost as well as we did on foot. Our war art even allowed us to invent fighting patterns for horseback that amazed Subai Tahn.

We hired an archer to teach us to use the bows we received from Kang's troops. We did not keep him around for very long because the art of archery is not very complex and takes mostly repetitious practice. Besides, Subai Tahn proved himself a great teacher in this area also, as his horse people were known the world over as the best archers.

When our archery teacher first arrived on Ravenhill, he said, "You men do know that archery is forbidden to all but imperial troops."

"Yes," I replied. "It is forbidden by the foreign Tardor conquerors. That implies no immorality in our practice of archery; only danger to us if we are caught. Furthermore, the Emperor allows certain warlords to employ archers in their troops with impunity. Our status as protectors of this region makes us warlords of sorts. Does it not?"

The archer retorted, "Certain warlords have signed treaties with the Tardor Emperor and are thus acting in his service. They may legally employ archers in the name of the empire."

"Are you afraid to teach us?" I asked.

"No," he laughed. "I hope the result of my work here will someday be Hahn arrows in Tardor hearts, but I want you to take the care of secrecy until that time."

Eventually word came to Bintu Village that a battle group from Warlord Kang's army was destroyed by demons, ghosts and dragons in the night. The few surviving troops who returned to the warlord were so terrorized that he could never use them in battle again. Kang swore than he would take vengeance on Sanjurra and its protectors after the harvest, but the harvest passed and he sent no troops. He swore again that he would destroy Sanjurra the next summer, but again he made no aggressive moves in the area. Year after year he threatened, but was always too busy or the stars were not right for a southern foray. He left a ninety-mile radius around Ravenhill free of his tax collectors and bullies. None of the neighboring warlords made any attempt to move in on us either. I always felt that the people of the area should have been somewhat grateful to us. Instead they feared us all the more; almost shunned us, except for the few who worked for us or had regular business with us.

The warlord's threats were not taken lightly by the Dragons. Not at first anyway. We built a wall around the crest of our hill and sunk a maze of secret tunnels and underground rooms beneath it. We even hired laborers and brought them in with blindfolds on their eyes so that they would not learn the layout of our underground works. There they were to dig and lay the stone where the quantity of work would have distracted us from our prayers, philosophical studies and the practice of Wind Fist. We stopped the construction just short of turning our hilltop haven into a fortress.

The horses allowed us to patrol our area and hunt for bandits and criminal gangs much farther than we previously did on foot. We hunted in black robes with the Wind Fist symbol on our backs. Bandits came to fear the symbol like death itself. One gang decided to sport the symbol on their clothes in order to intimidate rival gangs into submission. We sent their heads to the other gangs with short letters explaining that the symbol was ours alone. After that, nobody even dared to scratch the symbol into the dirt. Eventually we sold most of the work horses and each bought a good war horse. We also received some fine horses from defeated bandits who wanted to live. Our hostler, Renje, turned out to be a good breeder. He blossomed in animal husbandry after Subai Tahn died of a lung infection. The sale of fine colts and fillies provided more income and we used some of the extra money to hire two assistants for Renje.

Very occasionally, we would get visitors from Sanjurra. They always stopped at the foot of Ravenhill and called up to us. It was said that Korenda applied to have our banishment lifted before he died. The Office of the Provincial Imperium publicly castigated the Elder for his 'erratic sentimentality' in the matter. I wrote to my mother on a monthly basis and she dictated her letters to my uncle who sent them to me each month. I was able to send her a small stipend each month and she lived more richly than I or any of my Brother Dragons did. That is partially because of her sale of the farm and partially because of the Dragons' way of living frugally. We still had to raise some of our own vegetables and livestock and sometimes ran quite low on quality foodstuffs.

Then one day a stranger came to us on Ravenhill. He walked right to the top and knocked on our southern gate. I heard the knocking from my evening meditations with my brothers. I did not know what it was at first because nobody had ever knocked on our gate before. I left the chapel and mounted the wall to have a look. A tall, thin man, bent with age and covered in rich, silk brocade stood below me. Wondering what business a rich old man could have on Ravenhill, I ran down to the heavy wooden gate and swung it inward.

When at last I faced him he smiled and said, "I'm Torenju Drakkan, here to ask a kind favor of you and your Brother Dragons for my master, Dorak Enju of Paigen City."

I told him, "Please come in. I'll take you to Han Erh, our superior. May I get you something?"

"Water, please," he answered.

I led him into the front room of the practice hall. It was the nearest thing we had to a receiving room for guests. I said, "Please sit down and be comfortable. I beg you to excuse the crude conditions. We live a simple life here on Ravenhill."

"This is quite comfortable, thank you," the old man said as he carefully lowered himself to a cushion near the window lattice.

I left for the chapel. We had a large jar of cool water there for our meditations. I placed my hand on Han Erh's shoulder to rouse him. He followed me after I quietly explained the situation to him and I drew a mug of water for our visitor. We walked to the practice hall and I introduced Erh to the old man.

"How may we be of service to you?" Erh asked him.

"For the last eighteen years, my master has sent the richest caravans in the empire to trade with the western barbarian lords beyond the Himdahl Mountains. His caravans pass from Paigen City through three provinces, the Himdahl wild region, the northern passes and barbarian lands to reach the great border cities of Slovenia. As you must guess, we pay toll after extortionate toll to the regional warlords, plus great fees to our caravan guards. The guards too often prove unfaithful or even unscrupulous in their dealings with us. So my master has sent me to ask you if you would guard our next caravan to the western lands over the great mountains. The trip will take one year from start to finish."

Erh and I looked at each other, and the reluctance I felt showed likewise in Erh's expression.

"I wouldn't like to leave our home for a whole year," I said politely.

Then Erh asked, "Why did your master send you to us? We live a secluded and peaceful life here. Surely there must be thousands of willing warriors in the empire."

Torenju Drakkan raised his hands palm up and said, "Willing, yes, but none with your reputation for honesty and fearsome prowess in the war arts. There could be no other group of seventeen men feared by a powerful warlord with an army that is itself famously feared throughout the empire."

Erh thought for a moment and said, "I'm truly sorry, my friend. I will have to decline any service to your master. We live in peace here and do not want to be drawn into the outside world any more than we must to maintain the peace of our region."

The old man bowed and said, "My master will be most disappointed, but your lives are your own to live in the way that serves you best. It is my master's instruction that I leave you with this token of his apology for interrupting your day." He handed a golden coin to Erh and backed away bowing politely. The heavy coin covered most of Erh's palm. "I will rejoin my party at the bottom of this hill and make my way back to Paigen City with the sorrowful news. Live in blessed peace, my Dragon friends. May the sun shine warmly on your backs and rain fall gently on your gardens."

Erh and I stared wide-eyed at the gold in his hand. Erh managed to say, "Farewell, friend from Paigen. Travel in peace and safety."

Just as he reached the door, Torenju Drakkan turned and said, "Should you reconsider your decision, my master promises five such coins to each of you who guard his next caravan, plus three more upon the caravan's safe return to Paigen." With that he left and gently closed the door behind him.

In the fall of that same year I rode with Dorak Enju's caravan from Paigen City. With me rode Kor Den, Torin Feng, Kanu Rahn, Tenju Gen, Kavel Tom and my giant friend, Denju Rehn. We took turns bearing our banner at the front of the caravan. It hung free from the top of a twenty-foot bamboo staff. The banner was two feet wide and eleven feet long. It was black with two words glaring out in flame red; *Lung Tong*, meaning The Fighting Brotherhood of the Dragon. Beneath the words it bore a gold symbol of the Wind's Fist. We found that the symbol's reputation had spread much farther than we had previously guessed. One evening just as the sun disappeared behind the hills, a large and dangerous looking group of free warriors rode to within an eighth-mile of the caravan. They looked toward the banner and slowed their horses to a leisurely walk. The two armored men in front of the double column argued for some time while occasionally pointing toward the banner or those of us who were dressed in black. Then they turned off without a word and rode away. We never saw them again.

We came to a warlord's toll on the road to Denchu along the Baren River west of Paigen. Seven horse warriors rode out onto the road bearing a red banner with crossed white broadswords. They looked quizzically at our banner, which Denju Rehn held high and proud.

The bearer of the red banner said, "Bring forth your caravan master to pay for Warlord Vando's protection through this region!"

I spurred Lungshan forward and galloped up to the banner bearer's side. The warriors' horses shied and balked in the face of Lungshan's eager ferocity. I laughed and said, "We ask no protection from hireling boys on women's pleasure mounts." I noticed Lungshan subtly maneuvering himself for battle. He swung his haunches around toward the banner bearer and faced a bigger man who bristled with anger. I could not help smiling that the novice warriors failed to see what was happening. My brothers waited in the caravan for the unlikely event that I would need their help.

"Your insolence will cost you double. Now bring your master to the front!" the angry one screamed.

"Clear the path," I said. "Or shall I gently bump you out of our way."

The angry man's eyes and mouth opened comically wide just before he drew his sword and raised it high. Lungshan lurched forward and bit the man's sword arm, dragging him off his clumsy mount before kicking the banner bearer off his mare with his rear hooves. Four of the other warriors spurred their horses forward and drew their swords while the fifth remained where he was and drew an arrow from his quiver. I slapped the first rider from his horse with the flat of my broadsword on his forehead. Lungshan bit and kicked the next warrior's horse until it turned and fled against the wishes of its screaming, cursing rider. My mount whirled round to take me from the sword reach of another warrior that had maneuvered himself behind me. I leaned forward as Lungshan turned and we lunged into his horse. He screamed in pain as his leg was crushed between the two horses, then he raised his sword to strike my mount's neck. I blocked his sword up with my own and took hold of his sleeve with my other hand. I tried to yank him off his horse but his foot caught in the stirrup on the other side. Lungshan bit him on the back while he hung screaming and helpless over the side of his jittery mount.

One swordsman and the archer remained on their mounts. The swordsman backed his horse away from me while the archer took aim. I didn't know what to do. He let his arrow fly directly at my heart. I could almost feel it penetrate my chest before it reached me. I couldn't take my eyes off the deadly missile as it sped toward my chest.

Without thinking, I thrust my sword at the arrow and shouted, "Stop!" Whether through blind luck or divine providence, my thick brass sword guard blocked the deadly path of the arrow. It bounced straight back off the guard and fell clattering to the road. I ignored the painful stinging in my sword hand and acted as if I had intended to perform the miracle that had just occurred. "Now drop your weapons before I grow angry," I said in the most authoritative and confident voice I could muster.

The archer's bow slid from his hand and the swordsman hastily tossed his weapon to the ground. I motioned my brothers forward and waited in silence for them to reach my side. The dismounted enemy warriors retrieved their horses and helped their injured comrades into the saddle before mounting their own mares. They stared wide-eyed at the seven of us in black battle dress and neat formation before them. Our banner billowed gracefully in the gentle breeze as if in mockery of the weakness evident in the defeated soldiers.

I smiled politely and said, "Go to your warlord and tell him to send enough toys for all my brothers to play with next time. Or send even more and we will play for lives."

The riders rode off in the direction from which they had come. The banner man casually dropped Warlord Vando's banner in the dirt and rode away from the others in a different direction. None of them turned to look back at us.

The caravan resumed its slow march toward the west and Kor Den said, "Where did you learn to block arrows with your sword guard?"

Torin Feng added, "And when did you become such an actor? I don't think they knew you blocked it by accident."

"None of that matters," Kanu Rahn said. "I don't think they'll be back in force or otherwise. Good work, Jeng."

There were a few times on the caravan journey when we did have to fight. Some people just could not seem to comprehend the situation they were in when facing the Dragons of Lung Tong. We tried to educate them and intimidate them out of our way when possible, but some of them just insisted on being destroyed.

One evening as we traveled high into the passes of the Himdahl Mountains, we saw a foreboding sign on the trail. It came in the form of large magic symbols made of carefully arranged bones covering a section of our path. Near the bones stood a painted wooden sign, which read, *REALM OF ALZAK. Pass not without consent of the Toll Master.* Useless magic symbols adorned the sign and I had to strain to keep from laughing when I looked at them. Several of the caravan workers were afraid to cross the ideograms.

One handler said, "They are signs of black magic. Evil curses against all who would dare to cross them!"

As a child I once had believed in such things. "Garbage," I said. "Nothing more than carefully strewn trash on the trail." I dismounted from Lungshan and my Dragon Brothers helped me to kick the bones out of our path. We were filled with disgust that most of the bones used in the ideograms were human; a terrible desecration of the dead! The sun had dropped below the mountains by the time we passed the bony signs in the dirt.

At the appearance of the night's first star, I said to the caravan master, "Shouldn't we set our camp for the night before darkness makes it difficult?"

He replied, "The handlers refuse to stop so close to the place of the evil signs."

I objected, "Don't they think the maker of the signs will be even more angry at a deeper intrusion into the area he claims as his own?"

"As I told them," the handler agreed, "but they fear the evil spirits of the ideograms more than the wizard who made them."

I rode to Tenju Gen and said, "The caravan will not be stopping in this area. The handlers are too afraid of the ideograms."

He stared at me for a moment then looked at the sky and said, "Fools. Traveling wild passes in darkness is far more dangerous than hill-country wizards and their impotent spells. I'll travel ahead on foot with Kanu Rahn and Torin Feng to back me up."

He rode his war horse to a handler in the caravan and I returned to the forward point. Soon we were picking our way along by torchlight. Several times we lost the trail and found it each time only with a bit of luck. I would have worried for the three Dragons ahead of us in the darkness if Tenju Gen were not among them. Denju Rehn rode at my side, while Kor Den and Kavel Tom patrolled along the length of the caravan.

Suddenly a bright yellow fire flared up on a high rocky knoll to our right. A voice came down from the fire, saying, "Pass back the way you came and leave your goods behind! Only by this action will your lives be spared the wrath of Alzak!"

I saw a pair of dark figures leave the caravan and slip into the brush toward the fire. It was Kor Den and Kavel Tom. I figured that Tenju Gen was also winding his misty way toward the fire. The handlers flew into a panic. Some were beginning to unload the pack animals. The caravan master shouted for them to stop immediately and act like men.

I shouted toward the fire, "Send your fool magician down to me if he is not afraid!"

A hoarse voice came from close by in the darkness behind me, "I fear nothing."

Lungshan jumped forward and spun to face the wizard, which hid my own startled reaction.

"Dragons, here!" I shouted in our secret language as I gaped at the man who had managed to sneak up on me. He was clad in tattered gray and black robes with heavy black furs around his headdress and shoulders. A lean black tiger crouched at his side. Various implements of unknown purpose dangled from his belt.

"I'm here," Tenju Gen said from just behind the wizard.

The wizard gave no sign of a startle at all. He simply reached down and stroked the cat, speaking to it calmly in some foreign tongue. Without looking back at Tenju Gen, the wizard said, "Back yourself away from us. You are in my home."

Gen made no move or reply.

I could see a dark figure lurking in the shadows behind him. The figure came forward with another and I saw by the flickering torchlight that they were Kanu Rahn and Torin Feng. Torin flinched noticeably when he saw the tiger. For a moment I feared that he might turn and run.

The wizard said in a soothing, friendly voice, "I am but an old man in my own house in the hills. I am as *weary* of years as *you are* of travel at this late hour."

My hair began to tickle at my neck as soon as I heard the sound of his smooth words. Kanu Rahn looked suddenly at Tenju Gen with wide eyes. Torin Feng did not seem to be paying any attention as he methodically scanned our surroundings with his eyes.

"*Yes*," the wizard continued. "*You* good men *are tired* indeed, and the desire for sleep does *sink* slowly and comfortably *down* into your beings. But the caravan master will not *listen* to your wise counsel *as a friend* would in his own home. *You* must know that I *can bring no harm* and *wish* no harm but ask *for peace and rest*."

I laughed and said, "I hear the hidden commands in your words, deceiver. You have no power of fear or persuasion over us; for you are nothing but a beginner in the art of words if that is your best!"

Suddenly his voice changed and his hands moved up and down quickly as he called out, "Then let the emerging clouds of hell rain down upon you!" A flash of sparking fire exploded from the ground in front of him as Torin Feng instantly leaped behind Tenju Gen and Kanu Rahn. A black arrow whistled through the spot where Feng had been standing and buried itself in Lungshan's flank. Tenju Gen and Kanu Rahn turned to see Feng drop two black arrows from his hands and dart into the brush with sword drawn. They followed quickly as the tiger leaped for my throat. I instantly slid off the other side of Lungshan and the cat sailed overhead. I regained my feet just as it whirled around to charge. I heard the wizard scream behind me as Lungshan snorted and stomped in battle rage.

I slashed deep into the tiger's neck as I tried to dodge its attack. My heavy broadsword was instantly ripped from my grasp as the tiger passed. It caught my robes with a claw and jerked me off my feet. I felt like a helpless child and thought my end had come. The tiger landed on top of me and crushed the air from my lungs as we tumbled together. Its muscles were as hard as Lungshan's as it thrashed in bloody fury. Soon I realized my sword blow had been fatal and I thanked the providence of Heaven once again, though I was utterly unable to breathe with the huge cat across my chest. Foreign shouts and screams of agony faded into the background as consciousness drained from me along with my pain.

I awoke with the six Dragons gathered around me. Denju Rehn helped me to stand up.

I asked, "Is everybody all right?"

"Yes," Tenju Gen replied. "Lungshan killed the charlatan wizard. Look."

Torin Feng said, "I guess the stallion was not superstitious enough to fear him."

The man was little more than crushed flesh and bone in a pile of bloody rags.

I gingerly touched my right side with my left hand and said, "I think I may have a couple of broken ribs."

"But you killed a tiger alone in battle!" Denju Rehn said. "Chu Jeng the Iron-Fisted Tiger Killer!"

Tenju Gen said, "I think Torin Feng has earned the names Arrow Snatcher and Dragon Saver." He bowed low and added, "Thank you, Brother."

We removed the arrow from Lungshan's leg and I rode a pack horse for a month while we both recovered from our wounds.

A few more incidents enlarged our reputation on the trail and nobody bothered us on the way back. When we returned, Dorak Enju begged us to stay at his palatial compound and tell us how the journey went. He was overjoyed that no extortion was taken by the warlords or gangs along the way. He said another caravan would be heading out in about three months and he wanted us to guard it. My brothers and I were anxious to return to Ravenhill, but we said we would give his request to our more rested brothers at home.

As the years passed, Dorak Enju recommended the Dragons of Wulin to his merchant friends. We hired a fine young man of Bintu village to arrange all such work. We met with him in Bintu only once every month or so at first, but soon we had more requests than we could possibly fulfill. Senya Dain suggested that we occasionally rent our banner out to merchants. The rest of us thought it was a fine idea. Soon bandits and warlords came to fear the banner and wonder if the Dragons were present or if the banner merely represented them. Rarely did we have to venture forth to punish those who violated a rented banner in our absence. During the years that followed our first caravan trip for Dorak Enju, we stopped raising livestock and growing crops. We maintained our austere lifestyle even though we had enough income to live like princes. The years passed in peace and happiness. My head was the last to take on streaks of gray; yet even the oldest among us remained as spry and lithe as a young tiger. The Way of the Wind's Fist continued to grow in refined power. It seemed that never a day went by that I did not grow in knowledge and skill, even if only in some small way.

17 - TEACHING

It was in my forty-seventh year that Cheung Mun came to us on Ravenhill. Kor Den saw the old man first, wheezing and struggling up the hill toward our south gate. He ran down to help the man and I went to get Han Erh, to tell him we had another visitor. It was the first stranger on our hill since the visit of Torenju Drakkan and this man was just as richly dressed. Erh and I brought water to the old man, along with sweetened rice cakes and dried figs. We followed Kor Den and the stranger into the front room of the practice hall.

"Thank you, good Sirs," the man said, taking a cool mug of water in his shaking hands. "I beg your pardon for disturbing the peace of your home. However, I am driven to you by the greatest need of my life."

Erh and Den looked as puzzled as I felt.

The stranger continued, "Your reputation reaches throughout the empire, not just as supernatural fighters, but also as men of peace, justice and strength. It is your strength of mind and spirit that brings me here, as well as your strength of body and martial prowess."

Erh seemed to have trouble hiding his growing impatience. He looked at me then back at the silk-attired stranger and said, "We... ah... I am Han Erh. You are?"

"I am Cheung Mun of Sanghuei City," the man said, bowing with his hands folded in the tradition of the far south.

Han Erh's eyes grew wide as he said, "I have heard of you, Sir. Many years ago, I studied with Master Viendu Ben in your fair city. You were a great patriarch even then. Please, let us sit and talk."

We sat down on some cushions as Kor Den served the figs and cakes.

"I knew Master Viendu Ben," Cheung Mun said, wistfully. "He was a good friend."

"But even older than you," Han Erh said. "I understand by your saying 'was' that Master is dead now."

"Yes," Cheung Mun said, sorrowfully. "His funeral procession stretched halfway across the greatness of Sanghuei and no ill word was ever spoken in his memory. Many years ago Master Viendu Ben spoke to me of you, Han Erh of Sanjurra. He laughed at your uninformed quest, but said you were the most able student he had ever taught. Then through my distant friend in Paigen City, Dorak Enju, I heard your name again. Over the years, I heard more about the Dragons of Wulin and even hired your honorable banner a few times." The old man stopped talking and chewed on a dried fig. He seemed to be lost in thought.

Han Erh waited a long time before pressing the old man. "Sir?" he asked.

The old man gave a start, dropping a small piece of fig from his mouth.

Han Erh ignored the old man's fumble and asked, "How may we help you? You said you were driven here by great need."

"Oh, yes. As you can see, I am very old. I will die soon and leave my children a vast fortune of farms, villages, mines and mercantile territories. I have five beautiful daughters and one son of no more than ten years. It may be somewhat different here in the five lake region, but in Sanghuei, the vultures of opportunity will descend on my family after I die. They will take all and leave my children destitute if not dead. I want you to make my son a Dragon like you. Only then will he have the strength of body, mind and will to hold my financial empire together for my children and grandchildren after I die."

Han Erh stood up. His face was stern; yet betrayed no hint of any inclination in the matter. "Your request is not one to be taken lightly. You may stay on Ravenhill this night. My brothers and I will discuss your request. You'll have our decision in the morning." With that, he looked at Kor Den with an unspoken order and turning, walked out the door. I helped Kor Den to set Cheung Mun up in the little house shared by Denju Rehn and Amon Deng, since they were away with Cheng Ner guarding a caravan.

Erh gathered all the available Dragons in the practice hall. He called us to order by saying, "We have discussed the matter of teaching our art in groups and individually, but never all as one. Now the time has come for a decision. Will the Way of the Dragon die with us or will we pass it onto those who are worthy?"

"How could we teach our Path to ignorant outsiders?" Gar Jeng asked.

Kavel Tom answered him, "All outsiders are not ignorant beyond hope. We were ignorant outsiders once. Surely the Path would be easier taught than discovered. I believe we Dragons are the first seed of a great people who live among the mundane and wait unknowing for the Path of Dragons to call them to their destiny."

Rume Lak objected, "It's not a matter of ease of teaching or discovering those you say are destined for it. If we start teaching the Path to outsiders, one of them might betray our secrets to the Tardor pigs that rape our people. Do we want them having our kind of power?"

Kanu Rahn said, "The Tardor have their own war arts. They were obviously powerful enough to conquer our people in the time of our grandfathers. Should we not give our people a means of gaining freedom? Let us spread our Brotherhood carefully among those we choose."

Han Erh raised his arms and voice, "That's enough. We have discussed this for years. One fact remains; the Fighting Brotherhood of Dragons will die with us or grow on its own. Senya Dain has reached his sixty-fourth year. My Brothers, we are old men. You are probably all firmly set in the decisions you have made years ago in this matter. I will only offer you this; I have lived a rich full life because of the Path. Even in the times we went hungry or felt alone for lack of wives and children, I was rich in peace and inner treasure. The Path has enriched my life beyond the understanding of outsiders." He looked around the room, which had grown utterly silent. "I believe the spirit of God led us to discover the Path for a reason less selfish than the personal benefit of seventeen banished men. I have enough faith in the Path to believe it will remain a force of justice and peace after we are gone... if we pass it on. I will vote for teaching our art. If it comes to pass that the will of the Dragons is against me, then I will live by your decision without further comment. Will each of you swear to live in firm support of the decision we make together today?"

Each Dragon nodded his promise to support the collective decision of the Dragons. We wrote our preferences in the matter on pieces of paper and handed them forward to Han Erh. Eleven Dragons gave their approval to teaching the Path. Only three voted against teaching.

Han Erh counted the papers and said, "It is done then. The Dragon will live beyond our short human years."

A cheer rose up from about six of us. No words were raised against the decision.

Han Erh said, "Now we need to decide how the Path is to be taught to our first student, the ten-year-old son of Cheung Mun. Who will travel south with Cheung Mun to guide him safely home? Sanghuei lies far outside of our area of protection."

I said to Erh, "I will go with him and bring his son back here if you wish."

"Get ready to leave by tomorrow morning. We should be finished preparing our system by the time you get back with the boy."

Cheung Mun rode one of the few pleasure mounts we kept, while I rode Cyclone, the boldly aggressive colt of Lungshan. My faithful mount was clearly frustrated at the lack of fighting by the time Cheung Mun's son and I returned to Ravenhill. The boy, Cheung Nem, shied away from Cyclone whenever chance brought them close. He was a weak, thin boy of fair skin and large doe-like eyes. I could not imagine him ever becoming a Dragon because his spirit was even more frail than his body. I used my powers of Dragon speech throughout our journey to prepare his spirit for the study of Wind Fist. I had him stand in a horse stance every night at camp and encouraged him to build strength of body and will. My efforts were producing little discernible fruit in the young man. I did not grow frustrated, though. I kept faith that the seeds I planted in him would grow strong in the fertile soil of Ravenhill's warrior culture. Like Han Erh, I had great faith in the transforming power of the Dragon's Path.

When we crossed the great river and rode into Ravenwood, I thought Cheung Nem would faint with fear. He sweated and shivered, but did not raise a word of complaint. I let him sweat as a small rite of passage after we left the horses at the stables and walked the dark forest road up toward Ravenhill. As we emerged from the forest and the Dragons' whitewashed houses came into view above us, I spoke an internal word of prayer to raise the boy's spirits.

He shouted, "This is Ravenhill, just like you said it would be!"

"How do you like it?" I asked, discretely observing his wide eyes and beaming smile.

"It's beautiful! I can't wait to get started with my studies."

"You lived in a palace-like compound with your father," I chided. "How can you think Ravenhill beautiful? I must tell you that Ravenhill is not comfortable like your father's house."

His face contorted almost enough to lose the beaming smile. "It's…" He seemed overwhelmed by excitement. "I don't know. It seems like a warlord's fortress or a wizard's. I feel the power of the place. I used to play at soldiery with my friends when I was a child. Ravenhill feels something like that."

I knew then that I had succeeded in empowering his spirit.

Kavel Tom became Cheung Nem's primary teacher though we all played a part in his growth on the Path. He took a vow of secrecy before he began his study. That secrecy and the way we carefully guarded our teachings became a strong factor in our way of survival. We constructed three lower Storms to protect the upper ones and called them Rain, Thunder and Lightning. At first many argued against this, but even most of those who had objected came to love the lower Storms as much or more than the older ones.

Kor Den lectured the boy on the way of the crane. Amon Deng taught the boy the spirit of the tiger. Each Dragon took the boy aside and taught him his own particular view on the fighting arts or his animal specialty.

Cheung Nem learned the nine Storms of Wind Fist and the weapon dances only after he had mastered my own basics form, Zephyr. It was the unanimous decision of the Dragons in my absence, that Zephyr should come first in the study. Such was their faith in the power of strong basics. I was deeply honored by their faith and silently praised the name of Master Kanoh Feng. I hoped that somehow he could hear me from Heaven.

Cheung Nem passed through many formal testing ceremonies as he progressed in Wind Fist. We were amazed at his rapidly acquired skills. Though we sought to teach him as fast as his ability to absorb the art would allow, we were shocked at the speed of his progress. We all expressed our regrets that we had not started our studies in the Way of Wind Fist rather than in the arts we had originally learned. We marked an advanced point of Cheung Nem's study with the Dragonwell ceremony that Han Erh and Senya Dain developed. In that beautiful ceremony, he earned the Dragon surcoat. He wore it with profound pride. His martial prowess and strength of spirit increased dramatically after the Dragonwell ceremony. Soon thereafter he passed through the Guardian ceremony created by the ever-secretive Tenju Gen. After three years of study, the young man had finished the entire fighting system of Wind Fist, learned some of the Dragon's higher Path and shown prowess in weapons and horsemanship. We all felt that some ceremony or test should mark his passage into Dragonhood. The boy looked up to us as some sort of supreme warriors and still felt that he was not a Dragon. Somehow we also felt that his training was incomplete. Erh sequestered us in the old long-house to discuss the matter.

He began the meeting with these words, "We have given our student the best war art instruction in all the empire, yet he is not one of us. It is time we sent him back to his ailing father and I cannot help but think that we would be sending him back incomplete if we did nothing more with him. I suspect that you all feel the same as I do. In illustration of that point, I ask which of you would feel comfortable calling the fine young warrior a Dragon?" He looked us over as several of us averted our eyes while others resolutely shook their heads. "What more does his training require?" he asked.

"Send him out to kill some bandits," Amon Deng said. "He fights nearly as well as many of us already."

Han Erh spoke up sternly, asking Amon Deng, "How did you feel when you killed a man for the first time, Brother? Do you want to put Cheung Nem through that without necessity?"

"I felt great!" the Dragon answered. "He was a bandit swordsman coming at me with two infamous criminals at his side."

Several of us laughed.

I said, "Cheung Nem is not filled with the tiger's spirit as you are Deng. I suffered many nightmares after my first kill, even though he was an evil thug as was your first. Cheung Nem has led a pampered and sheltered life. I think it would be wrong to send him out on a specific mission to kill a man, thug or no."

Amon Deng grunted his disagreement and crossed his arms.

Senya Dain said, "There is some hidden wisdom in Brother Deng's words. The boy cannot be a true Dragon until he is tested in fire as we were. The test need not involve killing, but should not be an easy task to fulfill. Our perplexing responsibility is to devise the test."

We pondered his words in silence. Over the years, we had all come to deeply respect Senya Dain's wisdom, and not only because he was the eldest among us. I remembered that my brother, Dain, was tried hard in life before any of us began the quest. His was a trial of fire, set by Warlord Kang's criminals. The fire took the lives of his wife and children. It seemed that I could feel his thoughts. Then it hit me that Cheung Nem would soon have to deal with the coming death of his father. It would not be right to heap a killing upon him so close to that. Senya Dain turned toward me and nodded slowly. I heard his thoughts agreeing with me in my mind. There was no mistaking that he was reading my mind as easily as if I had spoken my thoughts aloud. My eyes widened and he smiled knowingly.

"Excellent!" I blurted out.

All heads turned toward me and Han Erh asked, "What is it, Jeng? Have you come up with an idea?"

"We are an awesome force to contend with!" I said, still marveling at Senya Dain's newly revealed mental power.

"Perfect!" Denju Rehn shouted. "Jeng is right. Cheung Nem should fight with one of us. If he can defeat a Dragon in non-lethal combat, then he deserves the title of Dragon."

"Yes," Trou Gom said. "Dragonhood is not something conferred upon a man. It is something he takes by right of conquest after he has fully conquered himself by embracing the difficult way of life we ourselves have embraced. In that, he would have earned the right to try. And I say that our Cheung Nem has earned that right by conquering the Twelve Winds of Wind Fist and loving the Way of the Dragon just as we do."

Kavel Tom said, "I think he can do it. He has made it to a level of proficiency that we have named Guardian and Sovereign Knight of Wind

Fist. It is time for him to pass through the fire and come out on *our* side."

Han Erh smiled and nodded. He said, "This will be the grandest and most solemn of our ceremonies. We should call it…" he paused with squinted eyes, then continued, "Embracing the Dragon; for it will be the passage from the useless, vain pursuits of mortal men into the excellence of Dragonhood."

One month later, we assembled in a hidden glade, deep within Ravenwood. Moonbeams slanted bright and stark into the glade. A fifteen-foot-diameter circle that we named the Dragon's Lair lay at the center of the glade. A low altar guarded the north end of the lair. To the east a wooden cross stood sentinel with a Dragon's black mantle and hood draped over it. The mantle and hood seemed to be watching over the proceeding as if to judge the worthiness of he who would be a Dragon. A large ceremonial drum rested near the cross along with three smaller drums and a higher-pitched wooden striker. Seventeen torches burned at the perimeter around us. Kanu Rahn stood in the Dragon's lair to defend the Brotherhood in full ceremonial robes. He wore a thick sash wound tightly around his waist. Cheung Nem would have to take the sash before a certain length of incense burned out. Kavel Tom and Cheung Nem walked side by side up to the end of the lair opposite the altar. We all bowed low as they made the Wind Fist salutation to each other.

Using his formal Dragon name, Kanu Rahn said, "Who comes forth to my lair? For I am Silver Wing of Ravenhill."

Kavel Tom answered him with equal formality, saying, "It is I, Jade Eye of Ravenhill."

"And who is it this venerable Dragon brings hence?" Kanu Rahn continued.

Kavel Tom answered, "It is the honorable Guardian of the secrets of Wind Fist, Cheung Nem, gallant Knight of The Way and my son to be."

Kanu Rahn then turned toward the nervous young Guardian and the questioning and testing of heart went on until Kanu Rahn threw back his hood and said, "Enter then and prove yourself worthy."

We all knelt and prayed silently for the safety of the defending Dragon and the Guardian. They knelt and prayed for the safety of each other. Then we all stood as Cheung Nem walked over to the cross and picked up an incense stick from a small cloth on the ground. He lit the stick and placed it in its holder to burn.

As Cheung Nem set fire to the incense, Kavel Tom prayed aloud for the righteous success of his Dragon son to be.

Cheung Nem responded to his prayer formally and with thanks.

The voices of the Dragons rang out deep and strong in affirmative answer to their prayers.

The deep rumble of our answer had not faded from the moist air when Gar Jeng, Trou Gom and Gis Erh started a rousing beat on the ceremonial drums. The trees seemed to dance with the beat as Cheung Nem strode toward the lair. I felt the war-passion of the drums calling me to battle. As Cheung Nem jumped into the lair, I felt myself remembering and longing for the battle against Kang's troops, so long ago.

Kanu Rahn kicked Cheung Nem out of the lair almost immediately. The young Guardian sprang to his feet and rushed back in without pause. Kanu Rahn tried to sweep the Guardian's feet out from under him. The Guardian staggered slightly, then answered the sweep with a shovel punch to Kanu Rahn's ribs and a sweeping claw toward the sash. The fight went on and on without a moment's rest. The sash was loosening inexorably, despite Kanu Rahn's formidable defense. Cheung Nem was told earlier by his Sire Dragon that if he let up for an instant, Kanu Rahn would tighten the sash and undo the desperate Guardian's work. But Cheung Nem kept the relentless pressure on the older warrior. Then Kanu Rahn knocked the Guardian to the ground and quickly reached for the sash to tighten it. The Guardian instantly wrapped his legs around Kanu Rahn's ankles and violently spun himself around. The movement threw Kanu Rahn to the ground and the Guardian flipped himself onto his opponent. Batting the Dragon's arms away and stepping on his neck, the Guardian grabbed the last intact loop of the sash and leapt away with it in his grasp. The sash unraveled with a loud flapping sound like a banner in a stiff breeze, but Kanu Rahn took hold of the end before it escaped him completely. He yanked it back out of the Guardian's hands, jumped to his feet and backed slowly away. The drummers slowed their beat with the change in the battle.

I was astonished at the look of resolve in the Guardian's eyes. I looked back at the tiny bit of incense left burning and realized how close my fellow Dragons and I had crowded toward the lair without knowing it. Kanu Rahn almost looked desperate. I could see that he clearly would not give up the sash without a worthy fight. The Guardian rushed the Dragon with a rapid series of punches and kicks. The attack did not let up in the normal time that most fighters would prefer. I recognized Senya Dain's teaching in the Guardian's relentless attack. Even though Kanu Rahn was a better fighter, the Guardian's relentlessness drove the Dragon to desperation. Soon Cheung Nem held the sash in his own hands as Kanu Rahn toppled backwards out of the lair. Cheung Nem stood panting and dripping with sweat as the drums pounded out their final beat and stopped. He looked at the smiling Dragons and we acknowledged that our number had grown to eighteen.

Cheung Nem walked to the altar and placed his new sash upon it. After his Sire Dragon, Kavel Tom, removed his own sash and placed it on the altar, they knelt before it with Kanu Rahn, who had done the same. They gave thanks in silence while the combatants regained their normal breathing. Then they all bowed low toward the altar. They stood up and put on their sashes. Kavel Tom and Kanu Rahn walked to the cross and removed the mantle and hood from it. They returned to the new Dragon and placed the mantle and hood on his head and shoulders.

Then they each placed a hand on his head and said together, "New Dragon, you shall henceforth be called the First of Ravenhill; First son of the house of Jade Eye. May your house be blessed with honor and strength, forever."

The New Dragon then prayed with his Sire Dragon and the defending Dragon as the ceremony dictated.

Again our deep voices thundered out from the glade in affirmation.

Kavel Tom and Kanu Rahn left the lair and walked separate sides to the place where the young Guardian had entered to become a Dragon. There they met facing and turned toward the Dragon's Lair.

The first son of Ravenhill stood within the Dragon's Lair and faced them as a proud new Dragon.

Kavel Tom said, "Now, my son, you stand within to defend our holy Brotherhood. We salute you as Brother and Dragon."

Then the three of them made a formal salutation toward each other as the rest of us cheered. The drummers started the beat again and we broke into a joyful outburst of congratulations for our new brother. When we finally settled down, we carried our equipment back to Ravenhill, singing battle hymns and marches all the way. The feast that followed was filled with joy and physical contests that lasted for three days. It took nearly a week for our overworked muscles to recover.

18 - BETRAYAL

Cheung Nem returned home and pleased his father by taking a strong and capable hand in the service of his household and financial holdings. What his father could not have realized was that Cheung Nem returned home as more Dragon than Cheung man. The young Dragon returned to us from time to time and sent us many students. He held his family's fortune together just as his father had wished. He held it until just recently when the Emperor had him and his sisters and their children murdered.

In the years that followed our teaching of the first student of Ravenhill, we led hundreds of young men on the Path to Dragonhood. At first it was only a few at a time, then they came in scores. Eventually we built two dormitories; one at the base of Ravenhill and one for advanced students at the top. Many of our young Dragon Brothers secretly taught the Way of the Dragon throughout the empire and brought their students to Ravenhill to embrace the Dragon. We held four festivals to strengthen our bodies and four solemnities in honor of the Son of God each year. Many Dragons came to celebrate those holy days with us. They brought news and sometimes requests for assistance with them. It remained ever the way of all Dragons to see that none of our brothers went without help in time of need. Thus banditry was abolished in some areas and reduced in most others. The trouble came when we began to make war against the regional warlords, but it did not come directly from the warlords, themselves.

It is generally understood that the Tardor conquerors took our land with the traitorous help of many of the Hahn Nobles. Many other Nobles merely stood aside and chose not to interfere with the invading armies in the hopes that the foreign powers would leave them to their fiefdoms and holdings after the conquest. That was before the rise of the additional warlords that plague our people today, but the same selfish, treacherous blood flows in their veins. The warlords ceased for recent time to look at each other as enemies because they had a new enemy; the Fighting Brotherhood of the Dragon. We discovered too late that they met together and then met with the Emperor and his chief advisors. The result of that meeting came in the winter of my sixty-first year.

We had buried Han Erh in the peace and seclusion of Ravenwood only three days before the destruction of Ravenhill. Five of my original seventeen Brothers were buried there before him. After Erh's death, the remaining Dragons unanimously declared me Singka, leader and Highest Honor of the Brotherhood. Many young Dragons had arrived to pay their respect to Han Erh, our first Singka, and pray for his immortal soul. Many more were on their way to Ravenhill from around the empire. Others were spreading the sorrowful news from place to place. What we did not know was that death of a different kind was on the way to Ravenhill.

Morgarn, a fine young Dragon of my house, arrived two nights after Han Erh's burial. He crept to the top of Ravenhill like a shadow under the stars as was ever his way. Making his path to my house on the hill, he quietly knocked on the door. It took me a while to wake up and a while longer to realize the gentle sound was the deliberate knocking of a visitor.

I cautiously opened the door and, after recognizing him, said, "Hello, Morgarn. Please come in. How have you been?"

"Hello, Grandsire," he said. "I have been well and happy until I heard the news of Master Han Erh's illness. On my way here, I heard that he had become a Dragon triumphant."

I nodded and let the truth of the young Dragon's words drive the sorrow from my heart. Erh was indeed a Dragon triumphant. He had lived in honor and followed the Dragon's Path without a moment of wavering. His mind and heart were always aimed at doing Heaven's will in this life and never lost his humble desire for the next. Never a day passed that he did not faithfully live up to his baptismal vows. I could hope with confidence that his spirit stood in the presence of God.

Then he startled me by quietly asking, "What of the imperial troops massing in the area, Grandsire? What are they doing here in such numbers?"

"What do you mean 'such numbers'?" I asked. "There has been an increase in imperial troops for a week or so, but the talk is that they are all heading north to deal with Warlord Weng's outrageous activities there. They say his troops have killed several imperial tax collectors and even stormed and massacred a rural garrison."

Morgarn replied, "I don't know what Weng has done in the north, but the troops are not heading there. I spied a large group of them just south of Ravenwood, on the north bank of the great river. They all spoke with the Paigen accent and talked of impending battle. The troops grumbled that their target was held secret from them."

I felt my stomach tighten as I told the young Dragon, "Paigen troops would have no reason to travel so far to the south and mass there for an attack on Weng in the north. Three Dragons have already told us of imperial troops gathering to the northeast and northwest. We thought they were massing against Weng as the talk has indicated. Now, though…"

"Perhaps the talk is all deception," Morgarn said.

I told him, "I know it's true that Weng has done the things he's rumored to have done. It's also true that the Emperor is ruthless enough to allow many of his own troops to be murdered for deception alone."

"What shall we do?" he asked.

"Come with me. Let's rouse three Dragons to patrol for imperial activity in the immediate area of Ravenhill."

After the three Dragons set out on patrol, I told Morgarn he could stay in the long-house with some of the other guests. I returned to my house and slept fitfully.

The next day passed without incident, unless the fact that no more Dragons arrived at Ravenhill could be considered an incident. The patrols returned at the first light of dawn with no news of anything out of the ordinary. We continued our grieving over Han Erh's death and made our prayers together at the setting of the sun. The chapel was packed tight with all the extra Dragons on Ravenhill, but their youthful spirit was strong and encouraging to us older Dragons. We left the lesser students in charge of Ravenhill as we prayed.

Long into our prayers, a young student burst into the chapel. The heavy doors slammed into those who were standing in the back.

Their quiet indignant protests were instantly stifled by the youngster's shout, "Sanjurra is burning!"

The throng of Dragons quickly emptied from the chapel and ran to the north wall. I ran up the spiral stairs of the north tower with Kavel Tom and Cheng Ner. When we reached the battlements at the top, I gasped at the size of the fires. There could have been no doubt in my mind that the whole village was burning. Even the outlying farms and houses were bright torches in the night.

Kavel Tom asked in shock, "Who would do this?"

Cheng Ner added, "And Why? Sanjurra is a peaceful village."

Then Kavel Tom pointed to the plain below us and shouted, "Look!"

A long line of imperial soldiers passed a flame from torch to torch. The arc of fire spread fast along a line that had to be three miles long in a semicircle around Ravenhill. We saw rank upon rank of the troops in the glow of the torches held by those in front. Mounted officers stood before them with bright war banners on their spears.

I ran to the inside edge of the tower and shouted to the Dragons below, "Prepare to defend Ravenhill! Bring all weapons to the practice circle at the center of the compound! Stack rocks on the towers and battlements."

The Dragons instantly moved as one. Drums began a martial beat on the plain below as harsh commands rang out. Thousands of feet joined the thunder of the drums as they stomp-marched their way toward us. The lower student dormitory emptied quickly and students fled to the top of the hill. We shut the south gate immediately after the last of them scrambled into our walled refuge.

I turned toward Kavel Tom and said, "They will probably torch the thatch of our roofs. Only the chapel and this tower are roofed in slate. We will have to fight until they reach us in number. Then we will kill as many as possible and flee into the underground through the floor of the north battlement room. From there we will make our way deep into Ravenwood. I doubt the imperial troops will venture far into Ravenwood even if they think any of us escape. Bring every barrel of fuel oil to the walls. As the enemy breaches our defenses, smash the barrels and make sure our people stay out of the oil. We will torch the oil as we escape. Spread the word to all the Dragons now and get some archers on the walls."

I watched the enemy stomp their way to the base of the hill as my people prepared themselves for a battle at terrible odds. There were no more than fifty-three Dragons and sixty students on Ravenhill. We faced what looked like an army of about fifteen-thousand imperial troops. The line tightened as it closed on us and its four ranks became eight then sixteen deep. The troops stopped at the base of Ravenhill with the cessation of the drums. Ben Jin and Rume Lak ran up to the top of the tower with nine Dragon archers.

"A lot of good our archers will do," Jin said. "We have no more than six-hundred arrows on Ravenhill."

"We will soon have more," I said, pointing at the line of enemy troops. "Look down there."

Archers stepped forward through the ranks of spearmen and swordsmen. They set the tips of their arrows to the torches and drew their bows, aiming high over the old battlements of our home. I felt no need to shout a warning to my people; for the twang of a thousand bows and the hiss of winged fire would call to them more sharply than ever I could. Soon I watched the arrows reach high in the starry sky above us. I was glad for the fire at their points; for the Dragons would be able to dodge them if they did not fall too close together. Six arrows clattered to the roof of the north tower as we dodged and deflected them with our swords. In a desperate effort to avoid one falling point of fire, Rume Lak nearly bumped me over the battlements. A young Dragon caught me by the mantle and pulled me back.

I drew a deep breath and asked, "What is your name, son?"

"Quick Fist of Second Forest Province of the Brotherhood, Sir."

"Very well, Quick Fist," I said. "You were named aptly. Into what house were you born?"

"The venerable house of Night Wing," he answered.

He was a Dragon of Han Erh's house; the house of Night Wing. It never ceased to astound me how strongly a Dragon's own tendencies showed themselves in his house, even many generations down. This young Dragon showed Han Erh's firm resolve and confidence. For one eerie moment, I thought I saw Han Erh looking out of the Dragon's eyes. His fiery gaze revealed a dangerous desire to fight for vengeance at any cost.

I said to him, "Stay close to me, Quick Fist. The plan is for escape, not death."

He nodded and picked up an arrow. It still burned as he inspected it for cracks. Then he set it to his bow, closed his eyes and murmured a word to himself. The twang of his bow was later followed by a single scream from the troops below. His companions let fly with arrows they picked up, some still flaming at their points. Another volley of arrows rained down on Ravenhill from the army below. We dodged and deflected as before while fires from the last volley rose into the night sky from the crackling thatch of our roofs. Three more volleys followed before the troops began to charge up the hill. Our archers vaulted deadly arrows into the wave of attackers. Many fell silent or screaming, but others rushed on past them. The heat from burning thatch around us was cutting through the smoke to singe hair and cause panic in the lesser students. Dragons shouted encouragement and instructions to their young charges in the compound below. My companions ran out of arrows quickly. Then we threw rocks at those imperial soldiers who drew closest to the wall. The rocks felled as many as had our arrows. When our rock piles disappeared, we ran down to engage in swordplay.

Imperial soldiers were already breaching the wall when we reached the bottom of the tower. I soon learned that imperial troops made easy work in swordplay. Quick Fist and I hacked our way through them alongside Ben Jin, Rume Lak and the other Dragons from the tower. Rume Lak skewered a flaming board fallen from the long house and ran to throw it in the oil near the western wall. About thirty imperial troops were crawling over the wall there. Before he reached the oil, a javelin slammed its way through his lower abdomen. He held the javelin steady as he staggered forward and dropped his firebrand into the oil at his feet. He fell and remained still just as the flames rose up and consumed the enemy soldiers. I rushed forward, but his body was lost to the flames that killed his enemies.

Another javelin hissed over the flames toward Quick Fist. He dodged to the side and caught it in his free hand before it touched the ground. Uttering a short prayer, he closed his eyes and muttered the silent word again. He threw hard and the javelin left his hand, flying almost the exact reverse of the path it had taken toward him. A distinct scream of pain and surprise rang out from the other side of the flaming wall. No more javelins came over that section of wall.

We turned from the burning, screaming men and engaged a group of partially flaming troops who had run through a dying wall of flames at the south gate. No enemy activity could be seen at the gate and wall nearest Ravenwood. Smoke from the fires began to obscure everything but the brightest of the flames. Rivers of oil flared up at every section of wall.

"Follow me," I choked as I made for the north battlement. The Dragons followed close behind me, coughing in the billowing black heat. When we reached the north battlement, a group of spearmen barred our way. Archers lined the wall above and many dead Dragons and students lay on the ground before them. We tried engaging the spearmen with our swords and found that they were expert war artists, not simple soldiers. A close volley of arrows drove us back from the engagement and took three of our number. Suddenly, Tenju Gen rushed up from our right and spit flaming oil on most of the spearmen at once. We quickly slew the flaming spearmen and the archers jumped over the wall just before Tenju Gen's second blast of fire would have engulfed them. Three spearmen remained and Tenju Gen burned them to the ground before they could flee from us.

Wiping his mouth with a rag, Tenju Gen threw his torch over the wall and said, "I think one of our own number may have betrayed us. I have seen further evidence than this tonight." He pointed toward the burning corpses that had barred our only escape; a secret door that only the Dragons and higher students could have known.

I moved forward with my sword in hand and said, "Let us get to the tunnel with caution."

We entered the battlement room and found the trap door that led down to the tunnels and hidden rooms of Ravenhill. It was held shut with short iron spikes, hastily driven into the wooden jamb. Just then, several men burst into the small room with drawn swords. We turned on them, but stopped our attack as soon as we recognized them as angry Dragons and frightened students.

A particularly large and muscular Dragon shouted to me, "Spearmen and archers turned us back. The whole place is in flames and arrows are raining down on the compound!"

"Stomp this door in!" I shouted at him.

More Dragons and students burst into the tiny room and packed it to capacity. The heavy Dragon jumped up and down on the door several times before it began to crack and groan. He continued pounding it with his feet and soon fell through, catching himself with one arm.

"Get your feet on the ladder," I told him. "Then climb out, quickly. I know the passages down there and will lead the way."

I sheathed my sword and scurried down the ladder to the musty darkness of our long unused tunnels. My compatriots began filing down after me and I led them down the narrow sloping tunnel past the side tunnel that led to the storeroom and on to the central meeting room. It was in the central room below the practice circle above that I expected to find trouble if any was to be found in the tunnels. Two other secret entrances and tunnels led to the central room, but from buildings that were then collapsing in flames. I wished I had some light. Instead I had to stretch out with my feelings and the heightened senses of a Dragon to test the place for waiting enemies. When satisfied it was safe, I followed the left wall with my hands and found another passage that would lead us through another room to the final passage and our escape. We followed the exit passage for three miles under Ravenwood. The air in the tunnel was free of smoke, but it was old and oppressive with wetness and the pungency of moldering stonework. The sweat of my compatriots came forward to fill my nostrils. The scent of blood came with it though none complained of wounds. At last we came to the secret door that would let us into the dark forest. The younger, stronger Dragons pushed the moldy door open and we burst into the fresh night air. Silence greeted us and the trees blocked out any light that would have reached us from our burning home to the north.

I sent Ben Jin and four Dragons to the stables to get some torches. I waited with the rest of the Dragons and students for others to come out of the tunnels. Those who found their way out were immediately challenged by the rest of us. They all identified themselves in the darkness. No imperial troops came out while we waited. Many Dragons and students came out. Cheng Ner and Kanu Rahn came out together. Kanu Rahn's left shoulder and arm were pierced by three arrows.

"He saved my life!" Cheng Ner said, lowering the bleeding Dragon to the ground and preparing to tend his wounds. "My back was turned to the wall while I was fighting a pair of spearmen, when he leapt behind me to block a volley of arrows."

He was interrupted by confused shouts ringing out from the tunnel.

I called in to them, "We are in the forest here. Follow the sound of my voice and tell us your names."

Nine sooty students clambered down the tunnel, shouting their names unintelligibly and almost ran into me. Torches could be seen making their way through the trees to the west of us. The bouncing flames indicated that the torch bearers were running toward us. I named a fighting pattern from the third Storm of Wind Fist and one of the torch bearers called out with the spoken lesson that went with it. His answer told me he was Ben Jin and the Dragons I had sent for torches.

Ben Jin ran to a halt next to me and said between panting breaths, "The horses are all gone. Imperial troops gave us these torches as they died. They wanted to flee from us, but were terrified of Ravenwood. We chopped their feet off and left them as if they were walking on the road. We set their hats between their feet as if they had fallen there. Then we dragged their bodies off into the forest so that any others who came to our stables would never doubt that Ravenwood is haunted."

I nodded at his clever thinking and said, "Ravenwood may well be haunted for years to come… by us. It will probably be our only safe haven."

Tenju Gen and I took torches and searched the tunnels and lower rooms beneath Ravenhill for stragglers. We guided them out to the others. Onde Tor, Rume Lak and Gar Jeng died on Ravenhill that night. Twenty-one young Dragons and thirty-seven students died with them. We learned much later that more than seven-hundred imperial troops were slaughtered that night and on the six nights that followed. After the sixth night they withdrew far from the ghosts, demons and Dragons of Ravenwood.

We intensified the secrecy of the Brotherhood and sent messengers out to all Dragons across the empire. We found that many had been ambushed and killed along with their families. By the ways of secrecy, keen awareness and readiness at all times, many of us managed to stay alive. Four years passed before we left the area and stopped haunting Ravenwood entirely.

As the years wore on, our numbers began to swell again and the Dragons demanded justice. It was not enough for them that every warlord who lived at the time Ravenhill was burned was brought before us and died at my hands.

I thought it strange that almost every Warlord tried to justify his actions with some version of the cheap excuse that *people do what they have to do.*

I told them all that people have to do things like sow, reap, eat and sleep. Enslaving, raping, plundering and murdering innocent people are not things that people have to do!

The Dragons now call for the death of the Emperor. We could do it easily… and start a bloody civil war resulting in more death of innocents. As the Singka and the last of the original Seventeen Dragons of Wulin, I counsel them to live lives of justice and humility instead. I do not know what the future holds for our Brotherhood, but I surely do not want it to die in a blaze of foolhardy glory.

Now, I have told you something about how I became a Dragon. Hearing about the Dragons of Lung Tong and our holy Path does not make one a Dragon. You must understand that I respect the secrecy of our Path, which is not for the eyes and ears of outsiders.

I wanted triumph and fame when I left Sanjurra as a boy of thirteen. Long before the end, I came to understand that fame and triumph bring only fleeting moments of satisfaction. My body will die soon and the fleeting satisfaction of my life's triumphs and glories will die with it, but the effects of my actions on behalf of others will live forever. That knowledge is enough for me.

— The final journal of Ironfist of Ravenhill
Dragon Year: 4267

Appendix: The Seventeen Dragons of Wulin

*The Dragon names listed below
are not all written into the text of the story.*

Amon Deng was probably the most ruthless and surely the most aggressive of the Dragons. He studied the Black Tiger system and the straight sword from Master Tienja Von in Gwongen City. His brothers knew him as *Red Fang*. He was 19 when he left Sanjurra on his quest.

Ben Jin is the comic, tension breaker and lifter of spirits among his Brother Dragons. He studied the Five Star Monkey Fist system and the staff under Master Koren Jang in Chulin City. He is called *Spear Tail*. He was 17 when he left Sanjurra on his quest.

Cheng Ner is named *Typhoon* by his Brother Dragons for his ability to throw a man through the air like the winds of a terrible storm. He studied the internal Pushing Hand system and broadsword from Master Traku Jen in Jangtoh City. He was 23 when he left Sanjurra on his quest.

Chu Jeng was the youngest of the Seventeen Dragons. He studied the Iron Fist system from Master Kanoh Feng on Lungshan Mountain. He is called *Iron Fist*. He was 13 when he left Sanjurra on his quest.

Denju Rehn was physically the giant of the Dragons and is called *Avalanche* by his brothers; for such was the force of his physical attacks. He studied the Tiger and Crane system under Master Kahl Sem in Gwongen City. He was 21 when he left Sanjurra on his quest.

Gar Jeng is called *Silent Scale* for his ability to slink around unseen and unheard. He studied the Coiling Serpent system from Master Denmin Rahn in Banzu City. He was 19 when he left Sanjurra on his quest.

Gis Erh was perhaps the most sudden and furious in his attacks. He studied the Leopard system and the saber under Gendra Ner in Paigen City. His Dragon Name is *Fire Wind*. He was 18 when he left Sanjurra on his quest.

Han Erh is called *Night Wing*. He is one of the oldest and best of the

Dragons. A tall, strong, handsome, steady, natural leader, he was accepted as guide and master of the Dragons without any elections or trials to that end. He studied the Southern Dragon system under Master Viendu Ben in Sanghuei City. He was 24 when he left Sanjurra on his quest.

Kanu Rahn is named *Silver Wing* by his brothers for his superb aerial attacks and maneuvers. He studied the Eagle system from the venerable Master Tienjin Kahn in the Iron Hills of Hujay Province. He was 20 when he left Sanjurra on his quest.

Kavel Tom studied the Mountain Long Fist system under Master Jao Mun in the Ganju Mountains south of Lungshan Mountain. His Dragon name is *Jade Eye*; for he was a master at using his powerful gaze to terrify an opponent, conceal his thoughts or give the impression that he would do something other than what he intended. He was 18 when he left Sanjurra on his quest.

Kor Den studied the Mountain Crane system, the spear and the steel chain under Master Sil Garn in Paigen City. He is called *White Wing* for his crane-like grace and wind-riding abilities. He was 21 when he left Sanjurra on his quest.

Onde Tor studied the Whirling Fist system and double broadsword under Master Draku Yen in Gwongen City. When sparring with weapons, no other Dragon could beat his whirling double broadswords. *Mace Fist* is the Dragon Name given to him for his whirling relentless fist and sword attacks. He was 17 when he left Sanjurra on his quest.

Rume Lak studied the Iron Monkey system and the oak cane from Master Han Li in Gansau City. *Cloud Rider* is his honorable Dragon Name. He was 20 when he left Sanjurra on his quest.

Senya Dain is called *Shadow Wing*; for the shadow of his wisdom, experience and relentless pursuit of excellence protected his brothers from the glare of the outside world and its glittering false promises. Of all Dragons, he was the oldest and most prone to the vices of rage and vengeance. He studied the Green Dragon system, the dart, the sling and the throwing coin under Master Cheung Erh in Paigen City. Of all the Dragons, Senya Dain was most respected after Han Erh. He was 30 when he left Sanjurra on his quest.

160

Tenju Gen is called *Forest Mist* and was the most secretive and awesome of the original Dragons. Though he would rather have died than bring the slightest harm to his brothers, he was the most feared in his mystical powers. He studied the elusive and mysterious White Dragon system, fire projection and the deadly slapping palm technique under a Master he never named and in a place he never told. After his death, younger Dragons started the rumor that he studied from a dragon spirit in some mist-shrouded mountains beyond the great sea that have never been tread upon by another human foot, before or since. He was 19 when he left Sanjurra on his quest.

Torin Feng earned and surpassed his Dragon Name of *Lightning Strike*; for his hands could not be seen when he used them for fighting. He wrote a voluminous and mystical treatise on speed for all aspects of being, which few of the other Dragons could fully understand though all studied it. The book was lost in the burning of Ravenhill. He studied the Praying Mantis system under Master Chien Dru in Bintu Village. The great Master of Bintu had already died when the Dragons took up residence on Ravenhill so close to the village. He was 18 when he left Sanjurra on his quest.

Trou Gom studied the Cobra system and double broadsword under Master Hong Jem in Gwenje City. His Dragon Name is *Golden Claw*; for his fighting form was as perfect and beautiful as gold. He was 19 when he left Sanjurra on his quest.

Made in the USA
Middletown, DE
24 June 2022

67712075R00097